CONTENTS

P5

P21

P35

P36

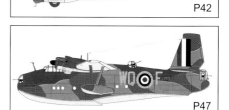
P40

P42

P47

P63

P91

Scale Aircraft Monographs
Camouflage and Markings
The Battle for Britain
May to December 1940
by Paul Lucas

Artwork by Peter Scott

Cover Artwork by Mark Rolfe

Series Editor: Neil Robinson

Design and layout: Steve Page

Published by
Guideline Publications
Tel: 01582 505999

Printed by Regal Litho Ltd.
352 Selbourne Road
Luton, Bedfordshire LU4 8NU

Reproduced here, and on the back cover, '**Duel**', by Geoff Nutkins, showing a Hurricane Mk I, P3878, YB•W of 17 Sqn., flown by P/O Harold Bird-Wilson in combat with a Bf 109E of 3./LG 2 in September 1940.

Prints available from:-
Geoff Nutkins
The Shoreham Aircraft Museum, 13 High Street, Shoreham Village, Sevenoaks, Kent TN14 7TB
Tel 01959 524416

THE BATTLE FOR BRITAIN

May to December 1940

ACKNOWLEDGMENTS

During the research for this book, I have received an immense amount of help from a variety of institutions and individuals both in Britain and the United States. Thanks are therefore due to:-

The staff of the Public Record Office at Kew; the RAF Museum at Hendon; Birmingham Reference Library; Dudley Public Libraries; the Midland Air Museum, Coventry, Warwickshire; Geoff Nutkins of The Shoreham Aircraft Museum, Sevenoaks, Kent; Roy Chrismas and the members of The Robertsbridge Aviation Society, Hurst Green, East Sussex; Mike Llewellyn of The Kent Battle of Britain Museum, Hawkinge, Kent; Tony Moor of the Brenzett Aeronautical Museum, Romney Marsh, Kent; Peter Turner and staff at The Spitfire & Hurricane Memorial Museum, Manston, Kent; the staff at the Tangmere Aviation Museum; David Campbell and members of the Lashenden Air Warfare Museum, Headcorn, Kent; Tim Staples and Sera Vine at Diverse Images, Brighton, East Sussex; Robert D. Archer, (whose knowledge of USAAC and USAAF colour schemes is unparalleled); Michael J F Bowyer, Dennis Knight, Michael Payne, Mark Rolfe, Peter Scott, John Short, Andrew Thomas and last but by no means least the series editor, Neil Robinson, without whom none of this would have happened.

After all the help I have been given by these people, any errors of fact or interpretation which remain are entirely my own.

Paul Lucas
July 2000

Unless otherwise stated, all the photographs used in this monograph are from the Andrew Thomas Collection.

Following the success of the first Camouflage and Markings Monograph, RAF FIGHTERS 1945 - 1950: UK BASED, the fact that the year 2000 marks the 60th anniversary of the Battle of Britain suggested to Guideline Publications that this would be an appropriate time to produce a Camouflage and Markings Special dealing with the colour schemes carried by RAF aircraft during 1940.

Over the last sixty years, the Battle of Britain has come to be seen as a defining moment in Twentieth Century British history in much the same way, and for the same reason, the Battle of Trafalgar became to be seen as a defining moment in Nineteenth Century British history. Both battles prevented Britain being defeated in a war against a major continental power, and whilst neither battle was decisive in itself, avoiding defeat at that time made it possible for Britain to continue the war until powerful allies could join the fight and ultimately prevail.

The year 1940 saw some of the greatest events in Europe, as the 'Phoney War' came to an end with the German invasion of Denmark, Norway, Holland, Belgium, Luxemburg and France. From Britain's perspective, the year is best remembered for the Dunkirk evacuation, the fall of France, the Battle of Britain and the Blitz.

Strange as it may now seem, at the time, the British Government, military, and public, seem to have been only dimly aware of the significance of the aerial fighting over Britain during 1940. This significance only began to make itself truly clear with the passing of time, and as the true nature of Hitler's Germany was revealed to the advancing Allied armies in 1945.

It was the British Prime Minister, Winston Churchill, who first coined the term 'Battle of Britain' which he used in a speech in the House of Commons on 18 June in which he said, "What General Weygand called the Battle of France is over. I expect the Battle of Britain is about to begin". In using this term however, Churchill seems to have been referring to the wider canvas of the war as a whole and not specifically to the air battles which were only just beginning to take place.

The now familiar title and narrative shape of the air battles over Britain during 1940 seems to have been defined by the Air Ministry decision to publish a publicity booklet for propaganda purposes on the subject. 'The Battle of Britain' a 34 page account of the air battle, was produced in March 1941. In this booklet, the author, Hilary St George Saunders, chose 8 August as the date the battle started and 31 October as the date it finished, and

Heading: Classic atmospheric Battle of Britain photograph - Spitfire Mk Is of 222 Sqn., landing at Hornchurch in September 1940. Note the Defiants in the background.
(Joe Crawshaw via Frank Campey)

Right: Another classic Battle of Britain image - the famous photograph of two Hurricane Mk Is of 501 Sqn., (P3069, SD·N and P3208, SD·T), taking off from Hawkinge in August 1940.

Left: Despite starting its RAF career as a medium bomber, quite a large number of Blenheim Mk Is and Blenheim Mk IVs, were modified to have four x 0.303 inch machine guns fitted in a fairing under the bomb bay doors, and were issued to both Fighter Command and Coastal Command as long range *fighters*. This particular Mk If, L8680, NG·Q of 604 Sqn is seen being put through its paces in June/July 1940, and looks as if it has had its undersurfaces repainted in-service in one of the 'duck egg' shades.

divided the battle into four phases; Phase I, 8 - 18 August; Phase II, 19 August - 5 September; Phase III, 6 September - 5 October; and Phase IV 6 - 31 October.

This pamphlet was enormously popular. Total sales being estimated at somewhere around fifteen million, with separate print runs and distribution in the United States and overseas. The interpretation which it offered was one in which RAF Fighter Command soundly defeated the German *Luftwaffe* and prevented an invasion. As Hilary St George Saunders later went on to co-author the three volume official history 'Royal Air Force 1939 - 1945' with Denis Richards, it is perhaps not too surprising that this is the view which came to prevail in Britain.

Both at the time and since, the battle was presented to the public as being a great victory which enhanced Britain's position in the world as a great power, with its people united and free to continue the war. In more recent years, as official documents from the time have been declassified, some historians have successfully raised serious doubts about the validity of this traditional perception of the battle.

This battle for national survival can possibly be said to have begun with the decision to withdraw the British Expeditionary Force from Continental Europe at the end of May, and to have lasted until the end of December, by which time it was obvious that the British people were not going to rise up and force the Government to sue for peace as a result of the night bombing of British cities - and Britain's impending bankruptcy had been avoided by the idea of 'Lend-Lease'.

When all these revisionist views are taken together, perhaps it is time to question the very term 'Battle of Britain'. It would appear that what took place in 1940 on the political, economic and military fronts, was not so much the Battle *of* Britain but the Battle *for* Britain, as the British Government faced the end of Britain's existence as an independent sovereign state. Hence the title of this book 'Battle For Britain: May-December 1940'.

With all the revisionist writing that has been done on the military, political, financial, and social history of the period, little if anything has been done with regard to the camouflage and markings of the RAF aircraft which fought the battle. In general terms, of the three operational

Commands which bore the brunt of the fighting, Fighter Command's contribution is well known, Bomber Command's contribution is less well known, and Coastal Command's contribution along with that of the Fleet Air Arm is usually forgotten altogether.

Whilst this present work only seeks to deal with the camouflage and markings of RAF Fighter, Bomber, and Coastal Commands, there is some information which deals in general terms with several of the other RAF Commands and the Fleet Air Arm to be found here. It is hoped to return both to this period and subjects, such as the Fleet Air Arm, in more detail in a later Monograph.

As with the more general histories of the events of 1940, the story of the camouflage and markings carried by RAF aircraft during this period is surrounded by myth and legend. The only possible way to try to cut through this was to start entirely from scratch using the primary sources held by institutions such as the Public Record Office, RAF Museum, and several smaller aviation museums, and a number of private individuals. These mainly take the form of Air Publications, Air Diagrams, Air Ministry Orders, DTD Specifications, files once held by the Air Ministry, Ministry of Aircraft Production, Royal Aircraft Establishment, and Operational RAF Commands, Works Drawings, contemporary publications such as 'Flight', and the remains of crashed aircraft salvaged by aviation archaeologists.

The result is not intended to be the final word on the subject, but aims instead to provide the aircraft enthusiast and modeller with a basic guide to what camouflage schemes and markings were carried and why, and to provide a basis from which further research can be carried out.

The nomenclature used in this book is

Above: The only 'film star' to appear in this book, this Vickers Weybridge-built Wellington Mk Ia, P2517, OJ·F of 149 Sqn., which featured in the wartime propaganda film "Target for Tonight". The undersides of this aircraft appear to have been finished in Special Night to specification RDM2 or RDM2A.

Below: Had an invasion actually taken place, Army Co-Operation Lysanders would have been employed in attacking the enemy with chemical weapons, or anything else that came to hand! This Lysander Mk II, P1684, UG·A of 16 Sqn is armed with two 20mm cannon which would have been employed against Motor Transport or light armour.

that of the documents consulted. Thus types of roundel are referred to by the terms used in Air Ministry Orders and not the Bruce Robertson notation familiar to most modellers. Proper colour names as given in AMOs and British Standard Specifications are begun with capital letters eg. 'BSS 381 (1930) No.1 Sky Blue', whilst colloquial names and references to a non specific colour, eg. 'pale blue', are in small type throughout.

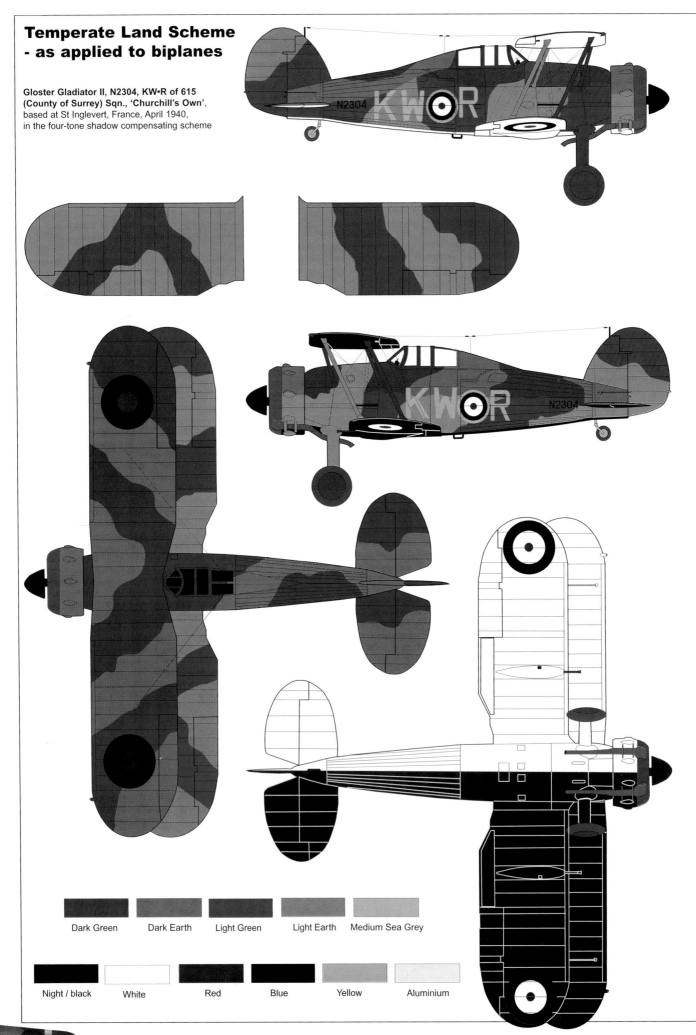

Temperate Land Scheme
- as applied to biplanes

Gloster Gladiator II, N2304, KW•R of 615
(County of Surrey) Sqn., 'Churchill's Own',
based at St Inglevert, France, April 1940,
in the four-tone shadow compensating scheme

Dark Green | Dark Earth | Light Green | Light Earth | Medium Sea Grey

Night / black | White | Red | Blue | Yellow | Aluminium

Early Hurricane undersurface scheme variations

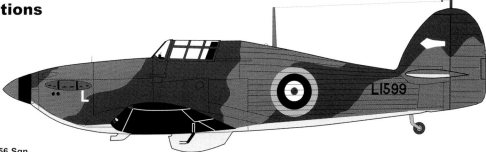

Hurricane Mk I, L1599 'L' of 56 Sqn.,
North Weald, 1938, with Night and White outer wing panels
and the original Aluminium finish down the centreline. Note
no underwing roundels carried.

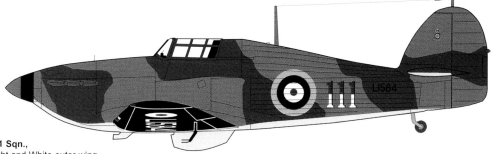

Hurricane Mk I, L1576 of 111 Sqn.,
Northolt, 1938, again with Night and White outer wing
panels and the original Aluminium finish down the
centreline. Note the underwing serial numbers and
roundels, and '111' fuselage marking in Red and White.

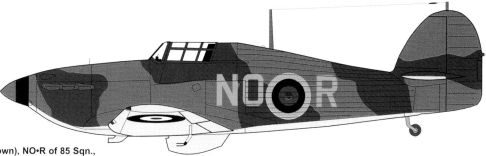

Hurricane Mk I, (serial unknown), NO•R of 85 Sqn.,
Debden early 1939. Note original Aluminium
undersurfaces and the toned-down White section of
the fuselage roundel. Underwing roundels in place.

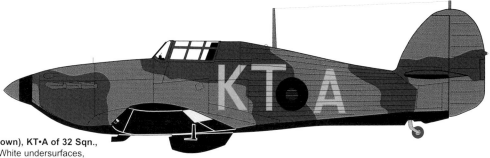

Hurricane Mk I, (serial unknown), KT•A of 32 Sqn.,
Biggin Hill early 1939. Night/White undersurfaces,
divided centrally down the centreline. Note that both
ailerons were left in the original Aluminium. Note
painted-out Red/Blue fuselage roundel and no
underwing roundels.

**Hurricane Mk I, (serial
unknown), NA•Z of 1 Sqn.,**
Tangmere, August 1939.
Night/White undersides of
mainplanes with Aluminium
nose, fuselage and tailplanes.
Note painted-out Red/Blue
fuselage roundel and no
underwing roundels.

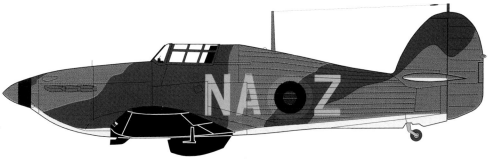

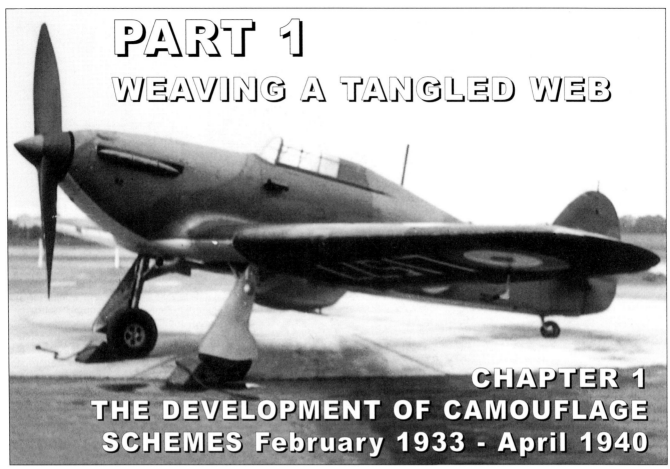

PART 1
WEAVING A TANGLED WEB

CHAPTER 1
THE DEVELOPMENT OF CAMOUFLAGE SCHEMES February 1933 - April 1940

For the most part, the camouflage schemes in which RAF aircraft were finished during 1940 were the result of a research programme carried out under the supervision of the Chemistry Department of the Royal Aircraft Establishment at Farnborough from 1933 onwards.

The Land Scheme

On 14 February 1933, the Air Ministry informed the Royal Aircraft Establishment that it had been decided that an experiment should be carried out at Farnborough to find a means of reducing the visibility of an aircraft when viewed from above when on the ground or in flight. The results of the experiment were submitted to the Air Ministry during the following August in an RAE report entitled 'Note on Colour Schemes to Decrease Visibility of Aircraft from Above.'

The report stated that it was not difficult to camouflage a fixed object such as an aircraft on the ground, because any

changes in the light affected both object and background it was viewed against equally. Problems were only likely to occur when seasonal changes in the background occurred, or the object was moved to another location. Fixed objects therefore could be camouflaged by applying a pattern of contrasting colours, one of which matched the background against which the object was viewed, which would alter the shape of the object and make it less easy to recognise from a distance.

An aircraft in flight however would be viewed against a background which would be constantly changing, as would the aircraft's distance from that background. The further away from the background and closer to the eye the aircraft is, the darker it appears. The atmospheric conditions prevailing at the time could also effect tonal values; for example shadows thrown by bright sunlight or the flash of light from changing angles. Some work had been done on aircraft

camouflage at Orfordness during the First World War which led to the conclusion that broad, irregular curves or stripes of highly contrasting colours, similar to the average background, which ran diagonally across the aeroplane gave the best results.

Using this knowledge as a starting point, it was considered that the factors which needed to be taken into account in designing a suitable camouflage scheme for an aircraft were:-
(i) The most suitable colours
(ii) The size of the coloured patches
(iii) The design of the pattern
(iv) The type of the Identification Markings
(v) The possibility of reducing shadows
(vi) The prevention of light reflection

The most suitable colours seemed self evident as against the average European background, various shades of green and brown would suffice. A range of colours, from a dark green to a light sand were applied to pieces of doped aeroplane fabric and compared with various backgrounds such as trees, grass, heather and sand. From these samples a number of colours were selected which harmonised with various

Heading: Early Hurricane Mk I, L1577 of 3 Sqn., circa late 1938, in the then new Dark Earth/Dark Green uppersurfaces, with Night/White/Aluminium undersides. (via Michael Payne)

Left: The first camouflage scheme to be evolved was for land based biplanes. This Gladiator, N2036, HP·B of 247 Sqn., in August 1940, is in the four-colour uppersurface Temperate Land Scheme for biplanes, consisting of Dark Green/Dark Earth/Light Green/Light Earth.

Air Diagram 1160 'Camouflage Scheme for single-engine monoplanes', was applied to such diverse types as the Spitfire, and the Lysander, shown here in the form of Mk II, P9056, OO·M of 13 Sqn.

backgrounds. Only a few of these colours were then chosen for the next stage of the experiment, to be applied to whole wings to find the most suitable size of coloured patch.

The work at Orfordness had revealed that small patches tend to blend together at a distance to produce an overall even tone. If the resulting even tone did not match the background, then there was no camouflage effect, and therefore except at very short ranges, large patches of colour were needed to break up the outline. It was also found that even with large patches of colour, at longer ranges the colours still assumed a somewhat neutral shade and an object could be detected by the contrast due to the differences in the amount of light reflected from it and other objects in the immediate vicinity.

The design of the pattern was also based on the work carried out at Orfordness and confirmed the earlier findings that the colour demarcation should run diagonally across the aircraft and be carried as far as possible through the fuselage, engine cowling, and tail without stopping at any important structural point.

Little consideration seems to have been given to the matter of the identification markings because the report makes no mention of them, but it seems that they were all removed from the upper surfaces with the exception of one of the upper wing roundels, and this was modified into the 'night flying type' using the dull night flying shades of red and blue.

It is not clear from the report whether the possibility of removing shadows refers to those cast on to the aircraft itself by parts of its own structure, such as that cast by the upper wing of a biplane onto the upper surface of the lower wing, or the shadow cast by the aircraft upon the ground, either when at rest or engaged in low flying. The only comment the report makes is that in bright sunlight, an aircraft could be detected by its shadow on the ground and no effective method of preventing this could be found.

The final point was that to avoid bright reflections from the aircraft, matt colours were very desirable, with both Nitro-Cellulose dopes and distemper materials and colours being tested.

Flight tests were carried out using a Fairey Gordon to refine the scheme, and on 21 July 1933, it was flown in company with three other machines which were finished in NIVO, PC10, and V84 Aluminium for comparisons to be made. Over a whole range of backgrounds, the camouflaged Gordon was more difficult to see. The combination of greens and browns admirably suited the trees, cornfields and dried-up vegetation of the summer months and the report

concluded that a number of machines operating in various parts of the country should be painted in the same scheme as that worn by the Gordon and observations made as to the value of the scheme in comparison with NIVO which had been judged the second best camouflage scheme after the new RAE scheme.

The Air Ministry was sufficiently impressed to order service trials of the new scheme in January 1934. These evidently took some time to arrange because it was not until mid June that Nos 4 and 111 Sqns received supplies of four colours called Dark Earth, Dark Green, Light Earth and Light Green to enable the service trials to commence.

Like the trials at the RAE, the service trials were considered to be successful with the camouflaged aircraft showing a marked superiority over the standard NIVO and Aluminium schemes. As a result, at the end of December, the Air Ministry ordered further trials of the scheme in the Middle East and ordered work to start on developing a similar sort of camouflage for a sea scheme.

It was at this time that the Abyssinian Crisis came about as a result of Italian aggression in Abyssinia, and there was a sudden need for some kind of aircraft camouflage for those aircraft sent to Malta to strengthen Britain's presence in the Mediterranean should the crisis lead to war with Italy. The RAE mixed and despatched to Malta, both land and sea camouflage colours, and the aircraft of Nos 22, 74, and 202 Sqns all received camouflage finishes of one sort or another.

The adoption of camouflage.

The difficulties being experienced with the Sea Scheme not withstanding, with the all round success of the work being done on aircraft camouflage, and its first operational use on Malta also being judged a success, the question of whether to adopt camouflage for the whole of the RAF arose.

The issue was debated at a conference held at the Air Ministry on 13 February 1936, to determine the policy with regard to the camouflaging of aeroplanes, chaired by the Air Member for Research and Development, Air Marshal Sir Hugh C T Dowding. The

general conclusion reached was that camouflage should be adopted, but for home based aircraft only. Of these, fighters and light bombers would only be camouflaged on the upper surfaces; whilst medium and heavy bombers were to be camouflaged all over with a plain dark colour on the undersides. No decision was reached with regard to maritime aircraft as the findings of the Sea Scheme trials were not then confirmed.

Once the decision to introduce camouflage had been taken, standards of the new colours were passed out to paint manufacturers and new material specifications were drawn up for both cellulose and synthetic based paints that would be suitable for finishing the new metal monoplanes which would shortly be entering service as part of the expansion of the RAF. Some thought was also given to the design of the camouflage pattern that the colours were to be applied to.

At the end of February 1936, anticipating that the findings of the conference would be accepted by the Chief of the Air Staff, the RAE was instructed to begin to draw up the camouflage schemes for the Fairey Battle, Bristol Blenheim, Armstrong Whitworth Whitley, Handley Page Hampden, and Vickers Wellesley. The Directorate of Technical Development suggested that it would be expedient if instead of preparing an individual design for each type, a generic scheme could be drawn up for a typical single-engined monoplane and a typical twin-engined monoplane.

Night undersurfaces

All the work on camouflage undertaken to this point had been for use on the upper surfaces. The development of a camouflage finish for the under surfaces of aircraft has its origins in the trials ordered in December 1934, to try to find an upper surface camouflage scheme for use over the sea. By October 1935, as the Abyssinian crisis was unfolding in the Mediterranean and Middle East, the RAE had begun trials of sea camouflage schemes in conjunction with RAF Coastal Area at the School of Naval Co-operation based at Lee-on-Solent. The AOC Coastal Area, Air Marshal Sir Arthur Longmore

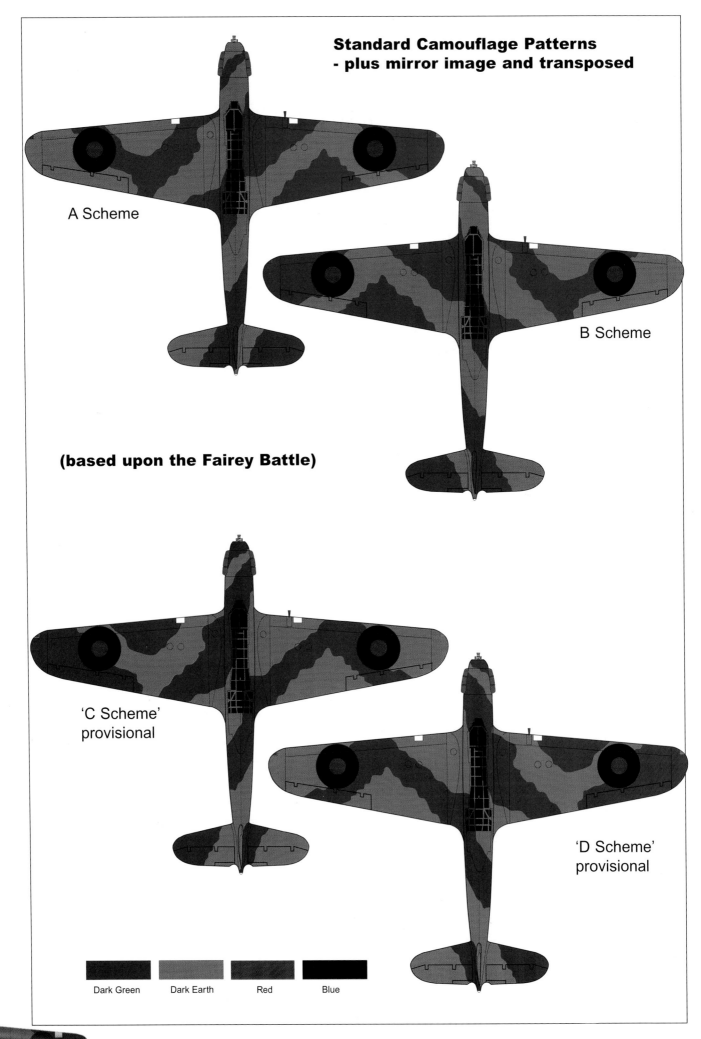

**Standard Camouflage Patterns
- plus mirror image and transposed**

A Scheme

B Scheme

(based upon the Fairey Battle)

'C Scheme'
provisional

'D Scheme'
provisional

Dark Green   Dark Earth   Red   Blue

was sufficiently impressed by the results of these trials to petition the Air Ministry for more trials of, "this most important subject", in a letter dated 3 January 1936. He then went on to express his opinion that further work was needed to come up with a camouflage scheme to render the lower surfaces of Flying Boats less conspicuous when caught by a searchlight or flare during night operations.

This matter was raised by Coastal Area's representative at the 'Conference to determine policy with regard to the camouflaging of aeroplanes', held at the Air Ministry on 13 February 1936, where it was suggested that Flying Boat under surfaces should be painted black. Whilst it was realised that this would make the aircraft more visible by day, concealment by night was considered to be more important. As a broadly similar view was held by the representatives of Air Defence of Great Britain who wanted a dark colour for the same purpose on the under sides of their new metal monoplane bombers, the conference decided that Coastal Area should carry out further experiments to determine a night flying camouflage for use on under surfaces.

Once the decision to proceed had been taken, the task was delegated to the School of Naval Co-operation in partnership with the RAE. The first trials consisted of doping the under surfaces of two aircraft, one with the then standard night bomber finish NIVO and the other with the new camouflage colour Dark Green. Both aircraft were then flown at night and illuminated with searchlights. Of the two finishes, the Dark Green was judged to be the less conspicuous of the two.

The RAE then carried out a series of small scale tests in the laboratory with a view to finding a matt surface which was less visible than Dark Green. A matt black finish, VBL 4. already existed, but whilst this had a very matt finish when freshly applied, the Carbon Black pigment was so soft that with a little rubbing it became glossy, and this was considered unsuitable if used by itself. However, the tests showed that mixtures of this Carbon Black and harder Ultramarine pigments produced a finish which offered not only low reflectivity, but were also quite durable. It had also been found that promising results could be obtained by adding black dye to an Ultramarine pigment. Therefore it was decided that for the second large scale experiment three experimental finishes, VBL 4 (Carbon Black pigment); Blue Black (made from Ultramarine and Carbon Black pigments); and dark blue (made up of Ultramarine pigment and black dye) would be compared with the Dark Green in a similar manner to the first experiment.

The results of this experiment were submitted to the Air Ministry in an RAE report during the first week of May 1936 which concluded that of the four finishes, the black and blue black were the most

effective. Of the two, the blue black, on account of its greater hardness, was considered the more serviceable of the two and no further developments were recommended.

On 8 May, the Air Ministry asked the RAE to submit twelve samples of 'Night' which were despatched on 26 May. On 10 June, the RAE received a letter which along with other matters suggested that besides the under surfaces, the new 'Night' shade would also be convenient for the identification lettering on the camouflaged upper surfaces and as an overall finish on the airscrews.

Air Diagrams

As a result of the work on aircraft camouflage undertaken up until this point, the first three camouflage scheme drawings which were prepared in June 1936 showed three colours - Dark Green, Dark Earth and Night, on three Air Diagrams, AD 1157 Camouflage Scheme for Twin Engine Monoplanes - Heavy Bombers; AD 1158, Camouflage Scheme for Single Engine Monoplanes - Medium Bombers; and AD 1159, Camouflage Scheme for Twin Engine Monoplanes - Medium Bombers. These schemes were applied to the Handley Page Harrow, Fairey Battle, and Bristol Blenheim respectively.

The next Air Diagram to be drawn up, AD 1160, started life as the Camouflage Scheme for Single Engine Monoplanes - Army Co-operation, intended for use on the Westland Lysander, in October 1936. However, work was proceeding apace on the new monoplane fighters and by November 1936, work on the Hawker Hurricane had progressed far enough for representatives of the RAE to visit Hawkers to discuss the camouflage scheme which was to be applied to the production aircraft. This was then followed by a similar visit to Supermarines in February 1937. These visits cumulated in the RAE submitting a drawing to the Air Ministry on 9 March 1937, entitled 'Camouflage Scheme for High Speed Interceptor Monoplanes'. It was suggested that this scheme would also be suitable for the Westland Lysander, so once the Air Ministry had approved the design, it was tidied up, and re-submitted on 25 March 1937 as Air Diagram 1160, Camouflage Scheme for Single Engine Monoplanes.

Whilst the now well known 'A' and 'B' schemes were illustrated by the Air Diagrams, it is of great interest to note that when the RAE was developing the schemes, they originally had letter/number combinations.

Designation L1 was what became the Temperate Land Scheme and in an undated Register of Aeroplane Camouflage Schemes which is believed to be from late 1937, which has been preserved in one of the RAE files held by the Public Record Office, the RAE's own designations are set alongside the Air Diagram numbers they became.

Air Diagram 1158 Camouflage Scheme for Single Engine Monoplanes -

Medium Bombers was that applied to the Fairey Battle and it has *four* RAE designations: L1A, L1B, L1C, and L1D.

AD 1157 Camouflage Scheme for Twin Engine Monoplanes - Heavy Bombers also has four RAE designations: L1F, L1G, L1H, and L1J

AD 1159 Camouflage Scheme for Twin Engine Monoplanes - Medium Bombers again has four RAE designations: L1K, L1L, L1M, and L1N.

Given that two of these designations can be accounted for by the mirror image which became known on the Air Diagrams as the 'A' and 'B' Schemes, presumably taken from the RAE designations which were applied to the Battle diagram which was the first to be drawn up, what is to be made of the two other designations? The most likely explanation is that they were originally intended to be not two variants of each colour scheme, one the mirror image of the other, but four. The 'A' and 'B' Schemes are well known, so it might be correct to call the other two the 'C' and 'D' Schemes. These would most likely have been identical to the 'A' and 'B' Schemes, but with the positions of the Dark Green and Dark Earth transposed. At least one Fairey Battle is known to have flown operationally during the French campaign in one of these transposed schemes.

Whilst the camouflage schemes for land planes were becoming established, trials with the problematical sea schemes had been continued. It was not until December 1938 that the decision to adopt, what the RAE then termed, Scheme 'S3' for home based flying boats was taken. This consisted of four colours, Extra Dark Sea Grey, Dark Slate Grey, Dark Sea Grey, and Light Slate Grey, and ultimately it became known as the Temperate Sea Scheme.

Early in 1939 Air Diagrams showing the Temperate Sea Schemes application to a number of different types of flying boat began to be drawn up. The types covered were the Short Sunderland on Air Diagram 1163; the Saro Lerwick on Air Diagram 1164; the Supermarine Stranraer on Air Diagram 1165; and the Saro London on Air Diagram 1166. All undersurfaces were shown as being finished in Night.

By the end of February, the decision appears to have been taken to finish the Sunderland upper surfaces in only two colours, Extra Dark Sea Grey and Dark Slate Grey although the whole of the under surfaces were to remain Night. Accordingly AD 1163 was amended during June.

At this stage it would appear that the finishing materials were to be to DTD 308, but on 25 July, the Air Ministry wrote to the RAE to say that there were at that time six Saro Londons and eight Short Sunderlands in service which needed camouflaging in accordance with their respective Air Diagrams. The Air Ministry pointed out that at that time the hulls of the flying boats were treated with Lanolin, a synthetic resin which served to retard corrosion. The Air Ministry proposed that the hulls should be camouflaged with a Lanolin solution pigmented to match the necessary colours and asked the RAE to mix sufficient materials for the purpose as soon as possible. By the time the materials had been prepared and despatched on 5 September 1939, war had broken out, and the Air Ministry had changed its mind as to the colour of the under surfaces. These had reverted to Aluminium for all flying boats instead of the Night finish indicated on the Air Diagrams, and on 7 September, the RAE was asked to prepare sufficient Aluminium pigmented Lanolin for the same number of aircraft.

With a growing requirement for pigmented Lanolin finishes, in March 1940 a new DTD Specification for matt pigmented Lanolin Resin finishes was issued, DTD 420. The specification named just the four upper surface colours, Light Slate Grey, Dark Slate Grey, Dark Sea Grey, and Extra Dark Sea Grey, apparently because Night had been dropped as the under surface colour, and the silver finish was obtained by over painting bare metal with a clear Lanolin which was already available.

Special Night
The beginnings of the development of this colour are slightly obscure. For some unknown reason, Professor T R Merton and Sir Henry Tizard visited the RAE sometime during late February or early March 1939. Whilst there, Professor Merton saw a copy of an ADEE report, No 928 which the RAE originally submitted to the Royal Engineers Signals Board of the War Department at Regents Park Barracks, which dealt with the visibility of a camouflaged aircraft when observed in a searchlight beam.

Apparently thinking better results could be obtained than those given in the report, Merton went away and produced a very matt black finish using a material called optical black which would seem to be the material used to line the insides of items such as binoculars. This sample was given to Tizard who in turn sent it to A H Hall, the Superintendent of the RAE, who in turn passed it to Dr Ramsbottom,

the head of the Chemistry Department.

The sample was returned to Tizard by Hall on 24 March 1939, along with a covering letter prepared by Dr Ramsbottom on the subject of matt black surfaces outlining the research work done by the RAE on this subject, and present state of the art.

On 28 March, A E Woodward Nutt wrote to Merton about his own visit to the RAE the previous Friday. In the letter, Woodward Nutt went into some detail of the problems encountered in producing an effective aerodynamically smooth anti searchlight finish. He considered that as the current Night finish absorbed ninety five percent of the light falling on it, so any improvement in the finish must be in trying to reduce the remaining five percent.

As at the time, none of the aircraft treated with the Temperate Land and Night Scheme were used purely as night bombers, any resulting improvement had to be suitable for both day and night operation. For this reason, the most obvious expedient, extending the Night finish up the fuselage sides and onto other parts of the airframe was looked on with disfavour because this would compromise the camouflage effect of the Temperate Land Scheme by day. Woodward Nutt also considered that any improved finish would have to take into account the need for such a finish to stand up to the wear and tear of service life whilst remaining aerodynamically smooth to the order of the surface roughness of not greater than the one thousandth of an inch then being obtained on production aircraft.

Because the latter two points were the major sticking points encountered during the development of the original Night finish, with the problem being of paint technology rather than physics, Woodward Nutt ventured the opinion that the best way of securing a really substantial reduction in visibility was most likely to be obtained by persuading the Air Staff to employ certain aircraft solely for night operations and to paint them Night overall rather than to increase the blackness of the parts of the aircraft painted in the current scheme.

In his reply the following day, Merton voiced his own opinion that he still believed that a substantial reduction in the amount of light reflected, especially at high angles of incidence would be possible if a small sacrifice in speed was considered worth while as this would reduce the chances of being seen and therefore reduce the number of casualties.

On 31 March, Woodward Nutt wrote to Merton suggesting that Merton should discuss the matter with Dr Ramsbottom and offered to arrange a meeting, contacting the RAE later the same day. He also appears to have raised the subject at the 47th meeting of the Committee for the Scientific Survey of Air Defence on 13 April 1939.

At this meeting the Committee learned that Professor Merton had been looking at the question of 'blackness' of the standard Night finish as currently applied to the undersides of bombers, and felt that if some of the current standards with regard to durability and smoothness of finish could be relaxed, a very much blacker finish could be obtained. The Professor then produced samples of metal painted with the standard Night finish and a blacker finish for comparison. He thought that it might be possible to produce a very black finish which could be applied quickly before a raid and which need only last for the duration of that raid. The resulting camouflage finish would thus be temporary and not compromise the the the daylight camouflage of the aircraft. It was pointed out that if a reduction in visibility from the air as well as the ground was required, it would be necessary to apply this finish overall instead of only the undersurfaces as at present.

After some discussion, the Committee recommended that in view of the importance of reducing the visibility of bombers at night, Professor Merton should discuss with the appropriate department of the RAE the practicability of producing a very black finish if the present requirements for durability and smoothness of finish were relaxed. In the event that such a finish should be evolved, the Committee also recommended that it should be applied to a service aircraft so that a comparison could be made between it and the standard finish as part of some night visibility experiments which were being carried out at Northolt.

Professor Merton's visit to the RAE seems to have taken place on 19 April, following which, some agreement was evidently reached, as on 25 April, Woodward Nutt forwarded to Dr Ramsbottom a sample of Professor Merton's dead black finish with the

The expansion plans of the late 1930s were weighted in favour of the bomber and the first Air Diagram to be published was AD 1157 'Camouflage Scheme for twin-engine monoplanes - heavy bombers'. This scheme was applied to the Whitley, the Wellington, (as shown on these two Wellingtons of 75 Sqn., one of which, AA•A, is P9206,) , and the Harrow.

Whitleys, such as these aircraft N1434, GE·E and N1460, GE·F of 58 Sqn., had the ultra matt, Special Night finish applied.

expectation that not only would the RAE meet the standard that it set, but would be able to surpass it.

Whilst the RAE got down to work on producing the new finish, the Air Ministry informed the AOC Bomber Command that two suitable bombers were to be firstly sent to the RAE for treatment, and then in in co-operation with Fighter Command, they were to take part in the night visibility experiments taking place at the Air Fighting Development Establishment at Northolt. By 6 May, Bomber Command had decided that it would be convenient for one of the aircraft of 38 Sqn., currently attached to ADFE Northolt, to receive the experimental finish.

Throughout May, the RAE obtained and tested several proprietary black finishes from the paint trade as well as several finishes prepared on site. Finally a choice was made, and on 6 June two Wellingtons were painted at Northolt. The first aircraft had the new experimental black finish applied to the whole of its undersurfaces and the vertical surfaces of the fuselage, fin and rudder. At the same time a second Wellington received a similar scheme but using standard Night.

Experimental work at the RAE continued however, and by 15 June a new 'Special Dead Black' had been produced which had greater light absorption than the experimental finish applied to the Wellington or the original sample provided by Professor Merton. A sample of 'Special Dead Black' apparently made from Nobels Monolite Fast Black was sent to Professor Merton on 15 June. In his reply to the letter which accompanied the sample, Professor Merton expressed his opinion that the new sample gave a very successful and satisfactory result on which any improvement was doubtful.

By mid August, trials of this new finish were being organised, and had just started when the outbreak of war came on 3 September. The trials were swiftly completed and found to be successful; and on 25 September, the Air Ministry wrote to the RAE to ask them to forward as quickly as possible 1000 gallons of Special Night to 3 MU for use by Bomber Command who were requesting that this material be adopted forthwith. Special Night was listed in 'AP 1086 the Vocabulary of Stores' under Stores ref 33B/ 299.

Aircraft Design Memorandum 332 Issue 2 September 1939

The advent of Special Night came too late for inclusion in Aircraft Design Memorandum No 332 (Issue 2) which was published on 8 September 1939. Entitled 'External Colour Schemes of

Spectacular Handley Page Harrow Mk II, of 420 Flight finished in overall Special Night. No 420 Flight was formed to pioneer the use of Aerial Mines as a means of destroying enemy aircraft at night. Note the 'sharkmouth'!

Aircraft', the memorandum set out for the benefit of the contractors, the requirements for those aircraft whose specification or contract called for the aircraft to be camouflaged or given any other external colour scheme. Airscrews were not covered as these had specifications of their own.

The under surfaces of bombers and torpedo bombers were to be finished in Night. The under surfaces of general reconnaissance land planes, troop carriers and bomber transports were to be finished in Aluminium.

Where any of the Air Diagrams showed two variations of the scheme, ie the mirror images of one another, the variations were to be allocated to aircraft as directed in the contract instructions.

Each of these Air Diagrams illustrated general requirements for each class of aircraft and the manufacturers had to adapt these illustrations to the specific type of aircraft being manufactured, the resulting design having to be approved by the DTD. These Works Drawings were to be fully dimensioned and specify which materials were to be used on metal and wood parts. Exhaust pipes and exhaust manifolds were not to be painted. Unless otherwise specified, training aircraft were to be given a glossy yellow finish all over their external surfaces.

The materials used were to be as follows.
a) For camouflage on metal or wood parts - Matt cellulose finishes or primer to Specification DTD 308 or matt pigmented oil varnishes and primer to Specification DTD 314.
b) For glossy finishes on metal or wood parts - Glossy finishes were required on the external surfaces of target towing aeroplanes, and on the yellow areas of training and target aeroplanes. The materials used on these surfaces were to

be either cellulose enamels and primer to DTD 63A or pigmented oil varnishes and primer to Specification DTD 260A.
c) For fabric parts - Doping scheme to Specification DTD 83A. When a glossy finish was required, a final coat of transparent varnish was to be applied.

Identification markings were to comply with the provisions of Standard Instruction Sheet No 4/Mod 861.

Camouflaged parts, ie those which were to be given a matt as distinct from a glossy finish which were to be delivered to stores or used as spares, were to have their external surfaces treated with the appropriate primer or red dope only.

Where reference was made to Specifications, Aircraft Design Memoranda, Air Diagrams, and/or Standard instruction sheets, the latest issue was implied.

The initial issue of the new camouflage finish Special Night was for the Whitley aircraft of 4 Group as these were the only dedicated night bombers in Bomber Command at this time. On 7 October, Bomber Command wrote to RAF Driffield, Linton-on-Ouse, Dishforth, Abingdon and the HQs of 4 and 6 Groups, instructing them that the Special Night was to be applied to the undersides of Whitley aircraft as soon as received, and asking the units concerned to inform Bomber Command when this had been done. By the end of October, Whitleys of 77 Sqn based at Driffield in East Yorkshire, had applied the new finish to some of their aircraft and had flown them in trials with searchlights. The reports on these trials were forwarded to Bomber Command on 22 November, and on 18 December, Bomber Command wrote to the Air Ministry to inform them that the undersides of Whitleys in operational squadrons had now been finished in Special Night.

CHAPTER 2
THE DEVELOPMENT
OF IDENTIFICATION
MARKINGS

August 1914 - April 1940

The identification markings carried by RAF aircraft during 1940 were the product of a lengthy development stretching back to the beginning of military aviation in Britain.

The principal means of identifying a British aircraft, as opposed to those of other nations, was by the use of the national identification markings which took the form of roundels on the wings and fuselage. This marking has a long history which goes back to 1914 when British military aircraft first went to war. When the original four squadrons of the RFC deployed to France in August 1914, military aviation was in its infancy, and the British Government appears to have devoted comparatively little thought to the subject of a national identification marking. As a consequence, the aircraft of these squadrons appear to have carried no national identification markings at all.

Operational experience soon showed that such markings were necessary as shown by a memo stamped, "HQ Military Wing RFC 2 October 1914", which stated "distinguishing marks have been found necessary. Union Jacks have been put on the lower surfaces of the lower planes. They are not large enough and larger ones are necessary". Following the introduction of this marking, it quickly became apparent that this was not such a good idea because the shape of the cross stood out much better than its colour, and it was therefore frequently mistaken for the German National marking which also took the form of a cross, albeit a black one.

Therefore at the end of October 1914, it was suggested that a system of circles similar to those used by the French be tried instead, but with a blue outer ring and a red centre. Once tried and found successful, the new roundel marking was introduced by HQ RFC Routine Orders No 76 dated 12 November 1914. In March 1916 a blueprint which sought to standardise the size and proportions of the roundel was issued to the aircraft manufacturers and AID. This set out seven different sizes of roundels, each one being of slightly different proportion, and this state of affairs seems to have persisted until the Armistice in 1918.

With the birth of the RAF as a separate entity on 1 April 1918, a flag was needed for the new service and all the designs submitted for consideration included a roundel which by this time had become the established National marking. The design for the RAF Ensign, finally approved by His Majesty The King on 9 September 1920, and was shown in a coloured drawing which gave the dimensions of the Ensign as 12ft by 6ft

Heading: Fairey Battles of 226 Sqn., at about the time of the Munich Crisis, October 1938. The original four-colour National marking roundel has been painted out and replaced with a two-colour red/blue 'wartime' roundel as advocated by the Air Ministry at that time. Visible serial numbers include K9176, G and K7709, O. (via Michael Payne)

Right: Although photographed during the summer of 1940, this Battle, L5080 of 142 Sqn., still carries the pre-war National marking roundels with which it was originally delivered in 1939.

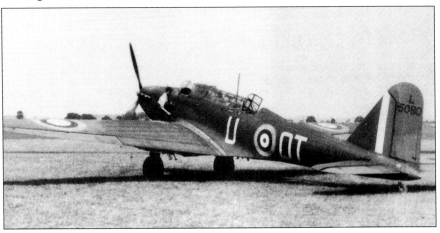

on which there was a roundel with a red centre 11 inches in diameter, a white band 11 inches wide, and a blue band 11 inches wide, thus giving a roundel proportioned in a ratio of 1-3-5. Once this design of Ensign was registered by the Heralds College, this roundel seems to have become the standard design for RAF roundels, and as such was to be seen on almost every aircraft used by the service from the early 1920s until the adoption of camouflage in 1936.

Prior to the adoption of camouflage in 1936, the only RAF aircraft not to use the red, white and blue roundel were night flying types which used a red and blue roundel created by extending the red and blue parts of the roundel outwards and inwards respectively to cover the area previously taken up by the white. This gave a roundel with a red centre 2/5ths the diameter of the whole roundel.

The roundels became enshrined in Kings Regulations as the identification marks for Air Force aircraft, but were supplemented by the use of three vertical stripes of red, white, and blue on the rudder. The rudder stripes first came into use under an instruction dated 7 March 1915, and Night flying types carried red and blue markings on the rudder. The original marking had blue leading, but this was altered to red leading in 1930, before being discarded altogether in 1934.

With the introduction of camouflage in 1936, some changes were made to the National markings. Firstly, the traditional bright red and blue were replaced by the dull night flying shades of red and blue; and secondly, a yellow outer ring was added to the red, white and blue roundels. The first measure, (of introducing these 'dull' shades), was taken to try to avoid compromising the camouflage finish, and perversely, the latter measure, (of applying a yellow outer ring), was made to make the camouflaged aircraft more visible(!), because, with the introduction of camouflage, concern was raised with regard to the risk of collision. So in an attempt to alleviate this concern, the yellow outer ring, which was to be equal in width to the other coloured rings of the roundel, was added to the red, white and blue roundels carried on camouflaged machines.

When the camouflage trials had begun in 1933, it was quickly established that the white ring in the roundel tended to compromise the camouflage finish, so the trials aircraft were flown with the red and blue night flying roundel in the dull night flying colours, and the Air Ministry decided to adopt the night flying roundel as the National marking for use on camouflaged machines in wartime. Thus, when the Munich crisis of September 1938 led to the majority of the RAF's front line aircraft adopting camouflage finishes, they also adopted the red and blue roundel on wings and fuselage as their wartime National marking.

With little improvement in the international situation in the closing

War experience quickly showed that the red and blue roundel, shown on this Lysander (above) of 2 Sqn., coded KO•M, was not prominent enough for identification purposes which led to the re-introduction of red/white/blue roundels on the fuselage sides as shown on this 142 Sqn Battle, K9274, QT•S, (below) photographed in the winter 1939/40. (via Michael Payne)

months of 1938, a conference was held at the Air Ministry on 20 December 1938, to discuss the question of aircraft markings at which it seems to have been decided to adopt wartime markings in peacetime. Thus on 27 April 1939, AMO A.154 - 'Identification Markings on Aircraft of Operational Units and Marking of Unit Equipment' was issued.

This AMO stated that it had been decided to adopt a standard system of identification markings on aircraft of operational squadrons throughout the whole of the RAF, both at home and overseas. As regards the National markings, these were defined as, (i) a blue ring surrounding a red centre which was to be located on both sides of the fuselage and on the upper surfaces of the wing tips; and, (ii) a blue ring surrounding a white ring with the latter surrounding a red centre which was to be located on the lower surface of the wing tips.

Fighter aircraft however were not to carry the National marking on the lower surface of the wing tips as the lower surfaces were to carry the special black and white identification marking. This latter point was amended by AMO A.298/39 which made an exception for fighters operating over France which were to carry red, white and blue roundels on the under surfaces of their wings.

The onset of war however quickly revealed problems with these identification markings. On 24 October a

section of No 602 Sqn was despatched on patrol following receipt of information that a convoy off St Abbs Head was being bombed. On reaching the reported position, the section found that a twin engined monoplane was flying low over the front of the convoy. It required close inspection to reveal that this aircraft was in fact an Anson as no National recognition markings were easily visible.

Following this encounter, the Section Leader put forward the suggestion that Coastal Reconnaissance aircraft on patrol over a convoy should be marked in some way which made them easily recognisable for what they were from a distance. The suggested method of doing this made at the time was of painting white strips on the wings.

The report on this incident and the suggested solution to the problem was initially sent to HQ Coastal Command, who forwarded a copy to Fighter Command, who in turn passed it on to the Air Ministry, adding its own suggestion that a yellow band might be applied around the fuselage.

Whilst waiting for some comment to emerge from the Air Ministry, Coastal Command did some experiments of its own which would appear to have consisted of applying red, white and blue roundels to the fuselage sides of at least one aircraft at Bircham Newton. The results of the trial were sent to fighter Command on 7 November. It had been found that whilst these markings aided recognition, they did not prove sufficient for fighter pilots during either an approach from astern or during circling manoeuvres. It was therefore recommended that, (a) red, white, and blue roundels be applied on the upper surface of the mainplanes of all General Reconnaissance aircraft in lieu of the present red and blue roundels; (b) similar roundels were to be applied to the sides of the fuselage; (c) the red, white, and blue roundels then in use on the silver under surfaces of General Reconnaissance aircraft were to be continued; and (d) if after a period during which these new markings were to be considered on trial, difficulties in recognition were still being experienced, a narrow yellow band on the upper surface of the mainplanes and the fuselage sides might be tried.

These changes were evidently forwarded to the Air Ministry where they met with approval as, on 21 November 1939, the Air Ministry wrote to all Air Officers Commanding to advise them that since the recognition markings on British aircraft had been set out in AMO A.154/39, war experience had shown that some of the markings described therein had been found to be unsuitable.

The letter then went on to list all the Signals which had been made with reference to this matter before going on to sum them up. All British aircraft were now to have red, white, and blue roundels on the sides of the fuselage; General Reconnaissance aircraft were to have red, white and blue roundels on top of their wings; and all British aircraft, (except fighters operating over Great Britain and night bombers), were to carry red, white, and blue roundels on the undersurfaces of the wings.

These changes in the National markings were incorporated in AMO A.520 which was issued on 7 December 1939. This AMO stated that war experience had made it necessary to alter the aircraft identification markings which were set out in AMO A.154/39. The alterations concerned the fuselage roundel on all aircraft and the upper wing roundel of General Reconnaissance aircraft which henceforward was to be of the red, white and blue variety.

These National markings remained in use, unchanged, until May 1940, when they were again revised. These revisions will be dealt with in a later chapter.

Serial Numbers

Contemporary documents refer to this marking by the terms 'Aircraft number', 'Registration number' or 'Serial number'. Whatever the term used, it refers to the number allotted to each individual aircraft by the Air Ministry, which served to give the airframe its individual identity. This marking was applied by the manufacturer

on the production line and stayed with the aircraft throughout its active service life. As there was no standard set of characters for this marking, the aircraft manufacturers went their own way.

In peacetime, the marking was applied to the rear of the fuselage, the undersurfaces of the mainplanes, and on the rudder, although the outbreak of war saw the removal of the underwing and rudder markings from all types except training aircraft.

The fuselage serial number which was common to all aircraft was to be 8 inches high, with individual characters not more than 5 inches wide and made up of brush strokes of 1 inch in width. This was to be marked on the fuselage of camouflaged aircraft in Night.

Identification letters and numbers

Following the decision taken in 1936 to introduce camouflage and the revised national markings with the yellow outer ring, the Air Ministry then began to consider the question of other identification markings. On 31 March 1936 the Air Ministry wrote to the RAE asking them to consider the question of identification markings on aircraft. The RAE was asked to consider which size, style, and colour of letters and numerals were best for recognition in the air.

The Air Ministry requirement was for a series of numbers to identify the squadron and a letter to identify individual aircraft within the squadron, all of which were to be visible at a distance of approximately 500 yards.

Because it was anticipated that it might be necessary to employ different coloured paints for recognition from the ground during air exercises, paints of three different colours were required. The Air Ministry was of the opinion that 'bright red' and 'lemon' were the most easily seen colours, and if this was confirmed by the RAE's trials, then a third colour was to be added.

The RAE was also to assess whether such markings had any adverse effect on the effectiveness of the camouflage scheme as a whole. When the trials were complete and decisions reached, a quantity of the three paints chosen were required for service trials in Air Defence Great Britain at the earliest opportunity.

Unfortunately, the RAE misunderstood what the Air Ministry required, and the first set of observations was made with reference to the 8 inch high serial number already being carried by the aircraft. It was not until the first tentative findings were sent to the Air Ministry in early May that the error came to light.

On 20 June 1936, the Air Ministry tried again by sending a further letter to the RAE pointing out that it was not the standard fuselage serial number marking which needed to be visible, but the squadron or code number on a camouflaged aircraft. The RAE was asked to determine (1) What size of identification letter, which was to be the individual aircraft marking, was necessary to be readable by the crew of an aircraft in flight at a distance of 200 yards under average conditions, and (2) what size of figures were necessary to be readable under similar circumstances at a distance of 500 yards.

The Air Ministry also pointed out that in practice, the squadron number would be on the rear of the fuselage and the RAE's trials should be carried out accordingly. The squadron number could be of one, two or three figures and the trials should include a three figure number as this was considered the most difficult to make out. Finally, the Air Ministry reiterated that three colours were required.

With the misunderstanding cleared up, the RAE got down to work and on 16 July 1936 wrote to the Air Ministry with its initial findings. Following preliminary tests with "the standard size letters and figures" using different coloured dopes, it had been found that it was not possible to identify any of the figures at 500 yards unless a very light colour, which compromised the camouflage finish, was used. The RAE therefore proposed to increase the size of the figures to 4 feet. It was then intended to find the darkest colours which would be visible at 500 yards, the proposed colours being grey, green, and red. Once this had been done, it was thought that the size of letter which could be seen in the selected colour at 200 yards could then be found.

The Air Ministry agreed to this course of action on 29 July 1936, stressing that

The sad remains of Miles Magister, P6377, of an unidentified Flying Training School, with the tailplane obscuring the fuselage serial number location, but showing the serial number repeated on the rudder. (via Michael Payne)

Code letters were specified to be in Medium Sea Grey and to be 48 inches high, as this Wellington Mk Ia, N2912, LG·G of 215 Sqn shows - although they could be smaller on aircraft with less available space. Note the fin flash, (introduced in May 1940), taking up the whole of the fin, and the non-standard fuselage roundel.

the RAE's final report was urgently required. Some measure of the urgency that the Air Ministry attached to the RAE's findings on this matter may be gauged by the fact that the Air Ministry wrote to the RAE in early September to badger the Establishment for its findings before finally receiving the RAE report which was dated 15 September.

The report showed that the three colours used were grey, dull red, and ident green. Two sizes of character were tested, the first being 48in high with 6in wide strokes, which were tested for visibility at 500 yards; and the second being 18in high with 2.5in wide strokes which was tested for visibility at 200 yards. Both sizes in all three colours were tested against an earth coloured background and a green coloured background, and it was discovered that the grey colour was the most visible in each case.

On 7 October 1936, the Air Ministry replied to the RAE stating that it had been decided to standardise upon the grey colour immediately. The RAE was therefore asked to prepare one hundred Standards of the new colour on metal, and a similar number on fabric, and forward them to the Aeronautical Inspection Directorate. The material was to be bought to Specification DTD 314 and was to be called Sea Grey, Medium.

When the new camouflaged monoplane bombers began to enter service however, no standard size or colour was adopted for the squadron or individual aircraft identification markings as each squadron went its own way. The Munich Crisis led to almost all such markings being removed or covered up, and it was not until the issue of AMO A.154 in April 1939 that anything approaching standardisation was achieved, with the introduction of the two letter code combinations to identify the squadron and the single individual aircraft identification letter.

The code letters were defined in AMO A.154 as being, "two letters to indicate the number of the squadron, which were to be located either forward or aft of the national marking on both sides of the fuselage; and one letter to indicate the individual aircraft, to be located on the other side of the national marking on both sides of the fuselage".

The code letters which were allotted to the squadrons were given in an appendix which ran to 650 squadrons, (far too many to include here), which were

Right - upper and lower: When code letters to identify Squadrons were introduced, the two letter combination could be placed on either side of the fuselage roundel with the individual aircraft code letter on the opposite side, as shown on these two 65 Sqn Spitfires.

in any case supposed to be changed on the outbreak of war. They were to be painted on with grey paint, Stores Reference 33B/157 in characters 48in high and strokes 6in in width. Smaller letters were only to be used when the lack of available space made such a course unavoidable.

There appears to be some question as to the exact colour of Grey 33B/157. At the time the code letters were applied, various observers reported them as being "light blue" including a report published in 'Flight' magazine. In the years since, this view has become discredited and it is now widely believed that Medium Sea Grey was used from the beginning. However, there is some circumstantial evidence, in the form of the terminology used, the numerical sequence of stores reference numbers allocated to various colours, and some archeological evidence, which, when taken together suggests that it might be possible that this is not the case.

The first piece of circumstantial evidence is the terminology used in the AMO, which calls for "Grey 33B/157", and not 'Sea Grey, Medium, 33B/157'. This might imply that in 1939, Stores Reference Number 33B/157 is not Medium Sea Grey at all, but a shade of grey paint which is already in service and therefore readily available. It is known that stores reference numbers could be, and were, re-allocated, so the 33B/157 of 1939 might not have been Medium Sea Grey at that time, even if it was so in later years.

The second piece of circumstantial evidence is that Grey 33B/157 appears to pre-date all the camouflage colours in the Vocabulary of Stores, even though Medium Sea Grey was not invented until after the colours of the Temperate Land Scheme. The earliest stores reference numbers for any of the camouflage colours which were developed from 1933 onwards, appear to be 33B/180-182 for Dark Earth, 33B/183-185 for Dark

Battle for Britain - RAF

There was no hard and fast rule on the style of lettering to be used on code letters. Compare the code letters on this 64 Sqn Spitfire, K9964, SH·W, with those of the two 65 Sqn machines on the previous page. (via Michael Payne)

Green, and 33B/186-188 for Night; all of which are to DTD 83A.

Unfortunately, the author does not have a complete stores list for this period, and one of the gaps falls exactly where it might be expected the Stores Reference Number for Medium Sea Grey to fall, somewhere between 33B/212 which is for the Dark Grey Primer to DTD314, (the last colour to be associated with the camouflage colours which are known to have been available to the Service by the end of 1938), and 33B/218 which is for Dark Sea Grey to DTD 83A, the use of which was only decided upon in December 1938. The earliest stores reference number found for Medium Sea Grey is 33B/345 which coincidentally (?) is to DTD 314.

The final piece of circumstantial evidence is to be found on the remains of Hurricane Mk I, P2728, preserved at The Kent Battle of Britain Museum at Hawkinge. At some point the under surfaces of this aircraft were painted a light blue-grey which it has been impossible to identify from any known colour standards. From a distance of a few feet, it gives the impression of being a light blue colour, but when seen up closer, it looks more of a grey. It might be that this colour was Grey 33B/157, but there is no hard evidence to either support or refute this. For further discussion, see 'Light Blue-Grey' in Chapter 12: Colours.

It is known that by 1940, the correct colour, Medium Sea Grey, was being used for identification letters as it has been found on the recovered remains of crashed aircraft.

Black and White special identification markings for fighters.

One of the most prominent identification markings carried by any British military aircraft during the period being covered in this book is the black and white identification marking carried on the undersides of fighter aircraft.

One of the major problems encountered in building the world's first integrated air defence system lay in finding some means of identifying friendly fighter aircraft, (a) to avoid them being shot at by anti-aircraft gunners, and (b) to allow them to be tracked by the Observer Corps. The need to have friendly fighters easily identifiable by anti-aircraft gunners was fairly obvious, but the need for the Observer Corps to be able to do the same thing was less so.

The requirement lay in the fact that the early Chain Home radar, transmitted its signals through 360 degrees, and in order for the operators to tell from which direction any returns were coming, the inland 180 degrees had to be blocked out electronically. This meant that there was no radar coverage inland, and all the plotting information which was required for a successful interception, such as the location of the fighters in relation to the raiders once they had crossed the coast, had to be obtained visually by the Observer Corps.

On 10 May 1937, Dowding wrote a letter to the Air Ministry in which he outlined an idea as to how friendly fighter

aircraft could be easily identified by anti-aircraft gunners and the Observer Corps. Dowding considered it essential that the undersides of fighter aircraft should be painted in such a way as to make them most easily identifiable from the ground.

His recommendation was that the underside of one of the lower mainplanes should be finished in silver dope and the other in dull black. The idea was that in what ever degree of light this arrangement was likely to be viewed, it would always present a characteristic

Left and above: Newly completed Hurricanes in early 1940, in the Night/White undersurface scheme, with Aluminium painted under cowlings and rear fuselage/tailplane undersides - a misunderstanding by Hawkers, as the actual scheme requested by Fighter Command was to have the entire undersurfaces divided equally, Night and White, down the centreline.

part coloured appearance to the observer.

By 30 June, this idea was being considered by the Air Ministry. The main objection seemed to be that an enemy could copy the marking and thus perhaps obtain some degree of immunity from the defences by doing so. However, there was also the view that an enemy would be unlikely to do anything likely to make himself conspicuous from below, and as all that would be needed to be done to implement the proposal on the fighters then being delivered or in service was to paint the underside of one wing black, a task easily carried out by the squadrons themselves, it was thought that the idea could be tried out. Accordingly, on 28 July 1937, the Air Ministry wrote to HQ Fighter Command giving permission for the painting of one wing of fighter aircraft black so that the idea could be tried out.

The experimental work with this form of marking was carried out at North Weald on biplane fighters and consisted of having the underside of one mainplane painted black and the other white. The ailerons were not to be painted due to the risk of the application of the new finish upsetting their balance, so the wing undersurfaces were not homogeneous in colour. It was found that in most attitudes of flight a part of the underside of the upper wing was visible from the ground and therefore a clear definition of the painted surface against the cloud and sky background was not obtained.

The experiment was considered to have had mixed results as when the aircraft were flying under unbroken cloud, or when they were viewed in the direction of the sun, the results were considered to be disappointing. However, when flying in a clear sky, or above scattered cloud, the marking was considered to be very distinct and was found to be visible to the naked eye at 12,000ft.

The overall conclusion seems to have been that the experiment had been a successes, and on 28 October 1937, Dowding wrote to the Air Ministry to inform them of the results of the experiment. At the same time he suggested that with production of the Hawker Hurricane gathering pace, the undersides of the wings of these aircraft, including the flaps and ailerons, should be finished black on the port side, and white on the starboard. He also suggested that to make the marking as clear as possible, the aircraft identification numbers should be omitted from the wing undersurfaces.

The Air Ministry agreed that some Hurricanes could be finished in this way for the purpose of a large scale service trial, and wrote to Dowding on 29 December 1937 to inform him of the decision. As production of the Hurricane

Right and above right: Two examples of unit applied Night/White wings over Aluminium undersides, this time on Spitfires. The aircraft opposite, is GR·W, possibly P9434, of 92 Sqn., photographed during the Dunkirk evacuation.

was well advanced by this time, it had not been found possible to apply the marking to early production aircraft, but it was be instituted as soon as possible without delaying production.

Whilst agreeing to the introduction of this marking, the Air Ministry however did not agree to the omission of the aircraft identification number from the under surfaces of the wings. It was felt that these markings should be retained because where disciplinary action had been found necessary in cases of unauthorised low flying, the offending aircraft was almost always identified by these numbers. That said however, authority was given to Fighter Command to delete the serial numbers from a number of aircraft not exceeding one squadron for limited periods of time.

In their reply to this, submitted to the Air Ministry on 5 January 1938, Fighter Command wished to be informed when Hurricanes with the new identification marking would become available so that a sufficient number of aircraft could be allocated to a squadron which could then remove the underwing identification characters for trial purposes. The letter then went on to take the Air Ministry to task for refusing permission for the markings to be deleted from all the black and white finished Hurricanes by respectfully suggesting that the relative importance of the two conflicting requirements should be kept in mind. This came down to what the letter termed "The negative desirable feature of identifying an occasional delinquent during peacetime", and "The vital and constructive operational requirement - the ability of gunners to identify fighters from enemy bombers".

With the decision made to apply the black and white marking to a batch of 50 Hurricanes, Hawker's Resident Technical Officer, (RTO), was advised of the fact in a letter dated 8 January 1938. The Air Ministry informed Hawkers that it was desired that the undersurface of the port wing was to be finished in black, and the undersurface of the starboard wing in white, with the flaps and ailerons

included in this colour scheme. The identification serial numbers under the starboard wing of the aircraft were to remain as they were at present, but those under the port wing were to be applied in white so as to be visible. The colouring which was proposed for the port side was not to actually be black, but Night. The appropriate DTD specification was to be DTD 83A.

The Air Ministry wished to be informed within the next two to three posts, of how quickly the alteration in finish could be made effective and what contract instructions Hawkers would require, (eg whether the change would incur extra cost). Hawkers were to note that the rest of the camouflage scheme was to remain unchanged.

In his reply, dated 28 January 1938, the RTO pointed out that it had not been made clear whether the outer wings only were to be black and white or whether the dividing line between the two colours should be on the centre line of the centre section. The sketch enclosed for Air Ministry approval showed only the outer, fabric covered, sections of the wings to be so coloured, and Hawkers quoted a price of £5. 0. 0d. for each aircraft to be finished in this manner. When the Air Ministry raised no objections, this is how the aircraft left the production line.

On 3 March 1938, the Air Ministry informed Fighter Command that the serial numbers of the Hurricanes earmarked for the new undersurface colour scheme

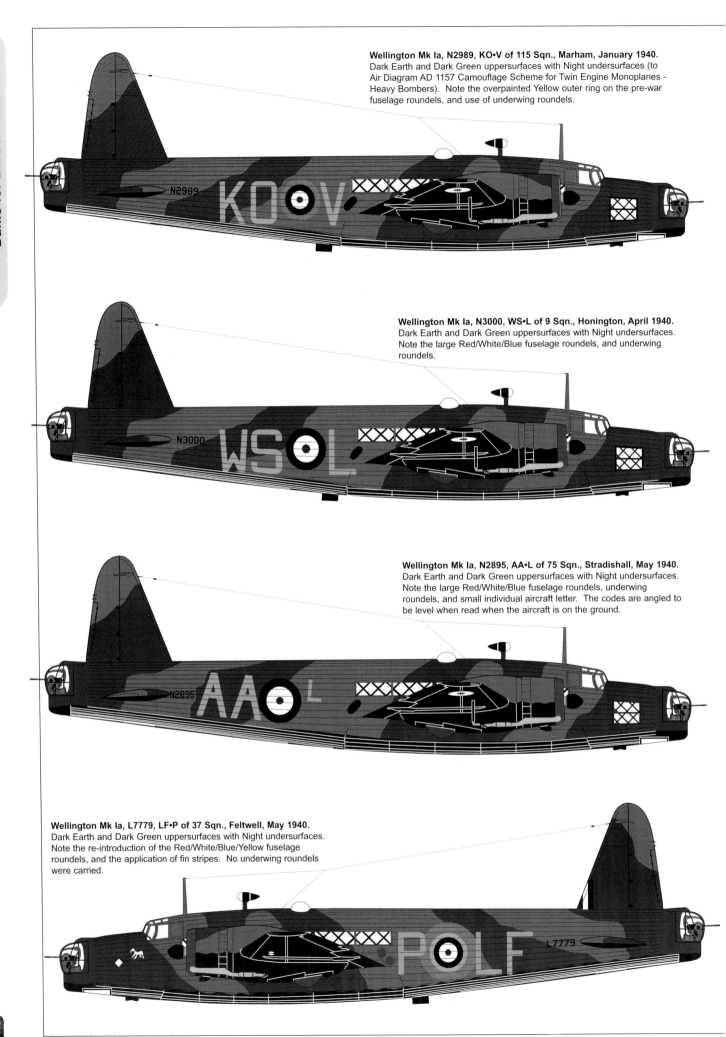

Wellington Mk Ia, N2989, KO•V of 115 Sqn., Marham, January 1940.
Dark Earth and Dark Green uppersurfaces with Night undersurfaces (to Air Diagram AD 1157 Camouflage Scheme for Twin Engine Monoplanes - Heavy Bombers). Note the overpainted Yellow outer ring on the pre-war fuselage roundels, and use of underwing roundels.

Wellington Mk Ia, N3000, WS•L of 9 Sqn., Honington, April 1940.
Dark Earth and Dark Green uppersurfaces with Night undersurfaces. Note the large Red/White/Blue fuselage roundels, and underwing roundels.

Wellington Mk Ia, N2895, AA•L of 75 Sqn., Stradishall, May 1940.
Dark Earth and Dark Green uppersurfaces with Night undersurfaces. Note the large Red/White/Blue fuselage roundels, underwing roundels, and small individual aircraft letter. The codes are angled to be level when read when the aircraft is on the ground.

Wellington Mk Ia, L7779, LF•P of 37 Sqn., Feltwell, May 1940.
Dark Earth and Dark Green uppersurfaces with Night undersurfaces. Note the re-introduction of the Red/White/Blue/Yellow fuselage roundels, and the application of fin stripes. No underwing roundels were carried.

Whitley Mk V, N1357, KN•H of 77 Sqn., Driffield, April 1940.
Dark Earth and Dark Green uppersurfaces with Special Night
RDM2 undersurfaces. Note the large diameter Red/White/Blue
fuselage roundels. No underwing roundels were carried.

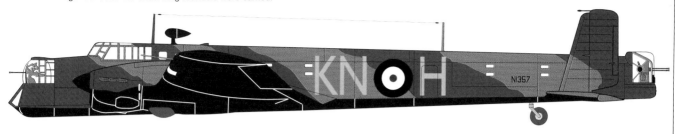

Whitley Mk V, N1380, DY•R of 102 Sqn., Driffield, April 1940.
Dark Earth and Dark Green uppersurfaces with Special Night
undersurfaces. Note the modified fuselage roundel, with the Blue
outer diameter of the large Red/White/Blue style overpainted in
camouflage colours, and the White areas reduced by overpainting
in Blue. At this time, the only dedicated Night Bombers in
Bomber Command were the Whitleys of 4 Group, which had their
undersurfaces finished in Special Night RDM2 and did not carry
underwing roundels.

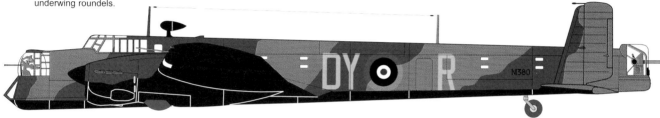

Hampden Mk I, L4074, KM•O of 44 Sqn., Waddington, April 1940.
Dark Earth and Dark Green uppersurfaces with Night undersurfaces.
Note the toned-down fuselage and underwing roundels and natural
metal (?) cooling gills.

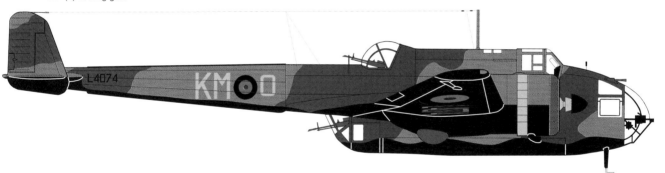

Hampden Mk I, L4192, ZN•K of 106 Sqn., Finningly, April 1940.
Dark Earth and Dark Green uppersurfaces with Night undersurfaces.
Note the undulating upper/under surface colour demarcation line on
this aircraft and the Hampden above. Natural metal (?) cooling gills.

| Dark Green | Dark Earth | Night / black | Medium Sea Grey |
| Red | White | Blue | Yellow |

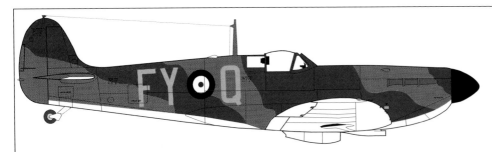

Spitfire Mk I, serial overpainted (?), FY•Q of 611 (West Lancashire) Sqn., Digby, February 1940.
Dark Earth and Dark Green uppersurfaces with Night/White undersurfaces. Note that the fuselage serial numbers were often painted over during this period and often re-applied in small 1 inch high characters at the top of the fin or rudder.

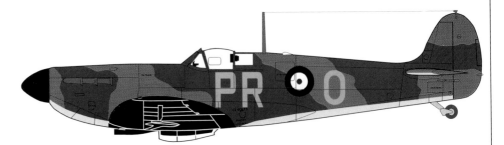

Spitfire Mk I, serial overpainted (?), PR•O of 609 (West Riding) Sqn., Drem, February/March 1940.
Dark Earth and Dark Green uppersurfaces with Night/White/Aluminium undersurfaces.

Spitfire Mk I, N3277, AZ•H of 234 Sqn., Leconfield, March 1940.
Dark Earth and Dark Green uppersurfaces with Night/White undersurfaces. Note the artwork on the cockpit access door flap, which became an unofficial Squadron marking, and appeared on many of this unit's Spitfires in 1940.

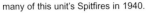

Spitfire Mk I, serial overpainted (?), LO•B of 602 (City of Glasgow) Sqn., Drem, April 1940.
Dark Earth and Dark Green uppersurfaces with Night/White undersurfaces. Note the name 'BOGUS' under the windscreen, and how the port fuselage roundel 'overlaps' the letter 'O' of the Squadron code, possibly caused by enlarging the diameter of the roundel.

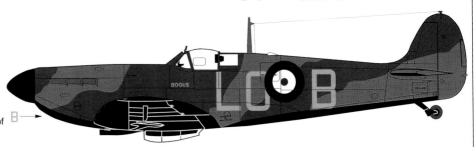

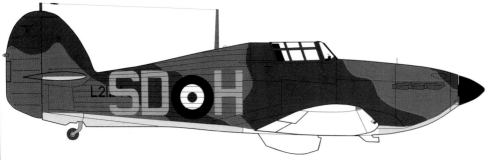

Hurricane Mk I, L2124 (?), SD•H of 501 (County of Gloucester) Sqn., Tangmere, early 1940.
Dark Earth and Dark Green uppersurfaces with Night/White/Aluminium undersurfaces. Note the slightly oversized Red centre of the fuselage roundel.

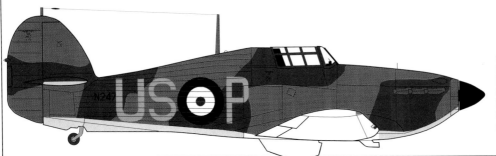

Hurricane Mk I, N2476 (?), US•P of 56 Sqn., North Weald, March 1940.
Dark Earth and Dark Green uppersurfaces with Night/White/Aluminium undersurfaces. Note the correctly proportioned fuselage roundel.

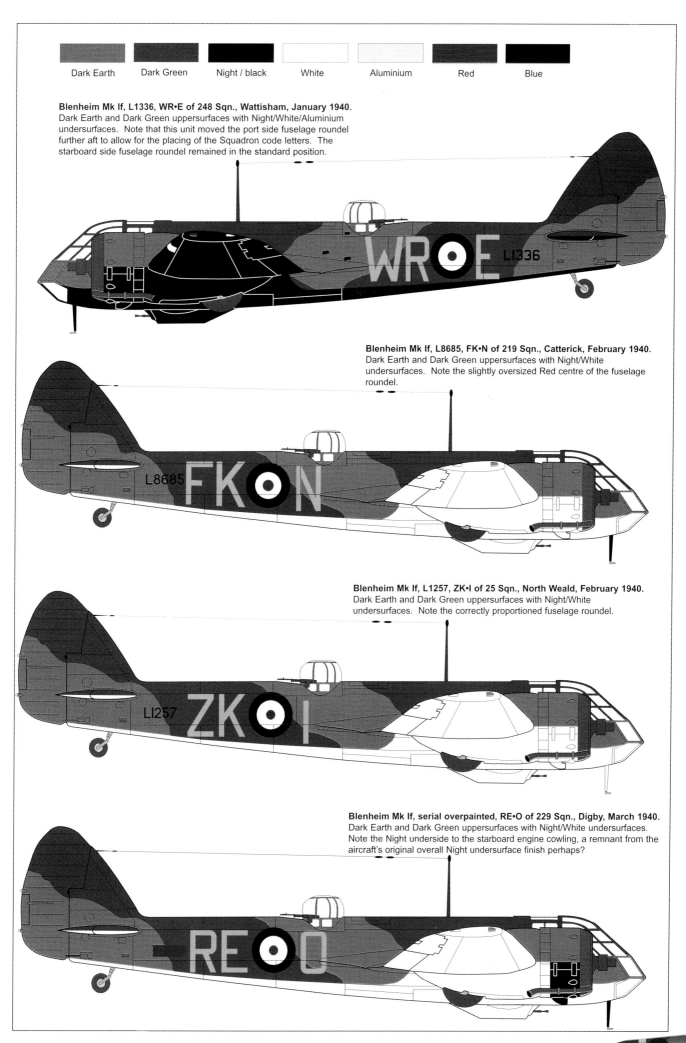

Dark Earth   **Dark Green**   **Night / black**   **White**   **Aluminium**   **Red**   **Blue**

Blenheim Mk If, L1336, WR•E of 248 Sqn., Wattisham, January 1940.
Dark Earth and Dark Green uppersurfaces with Night/White/Aluminium undersurfaces. Note that this unit moved the port side fuselage roundel further aft to allow for the placing of the Squadron code letters. The starboard side fuselage roundel remained in the standard position.

Blenheim Mk If, L8685, FK•N of 219 Sqn., Catterick, February 1940.
Dark Earth and Dark Green uppersurfaces with Night/White undersurfaces. Note the slightly oversized Red centre of the fuselage roundel.

Blenheim Mk If, L1257, ZK•I of 25 Sqn., North Weald, February 1940.
Dark Earth and Dark Green uppersurfaces with Night/White undersurfaces. Note the correctly proportioned fuselage roundel.

Blenheim Mk If, serial overpainted, RE•O of 229 Sqn., Digby, March 1940.
Dark Earth and Dark Green uppersurfaces with Night/White undersurfaces. Note the Night underside to the starboard engine cowling, a remnant from the aircraft's original overall Night undersurface finish perhaps?

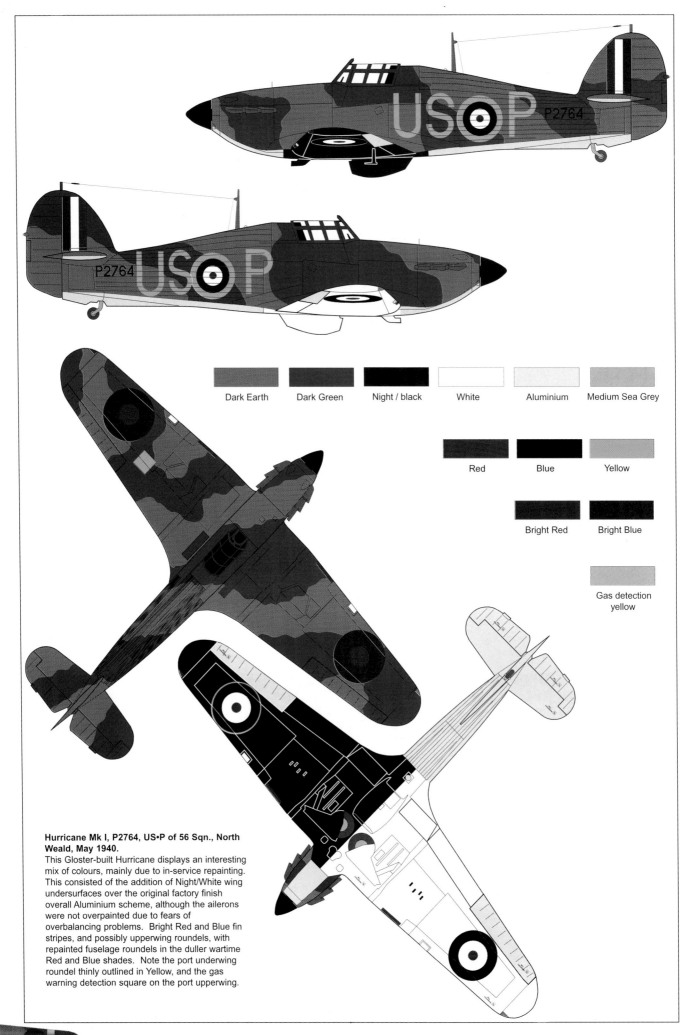

Dark Earth Dark Green Night / black White Aluminium Medium Sea Grey

Red Blue Yellow

Bright Red Bright Blue

Gas detection yellow

Hurricane Mk I, P2764, US•P of 56 Sqn., North Weald, May 1940.
This Gloster-built Hurricane displays an interesting mix of colours, mainly due to in-service repainting. This consisted of the addition of Night/White wing undersurfaces over the original factory finish overall Aluminium scheme, although the ailerons were not overpainted due to fears of overbalancing problems. Bright Red and Blue fin stripes, and possibly upperwing roundels, with repainted fuselage roundels in the duller wartime Red and Blue shades. Note the port underwing roundel thinly outlined in Yellow, and the gas warning detection square on the port upperwing.

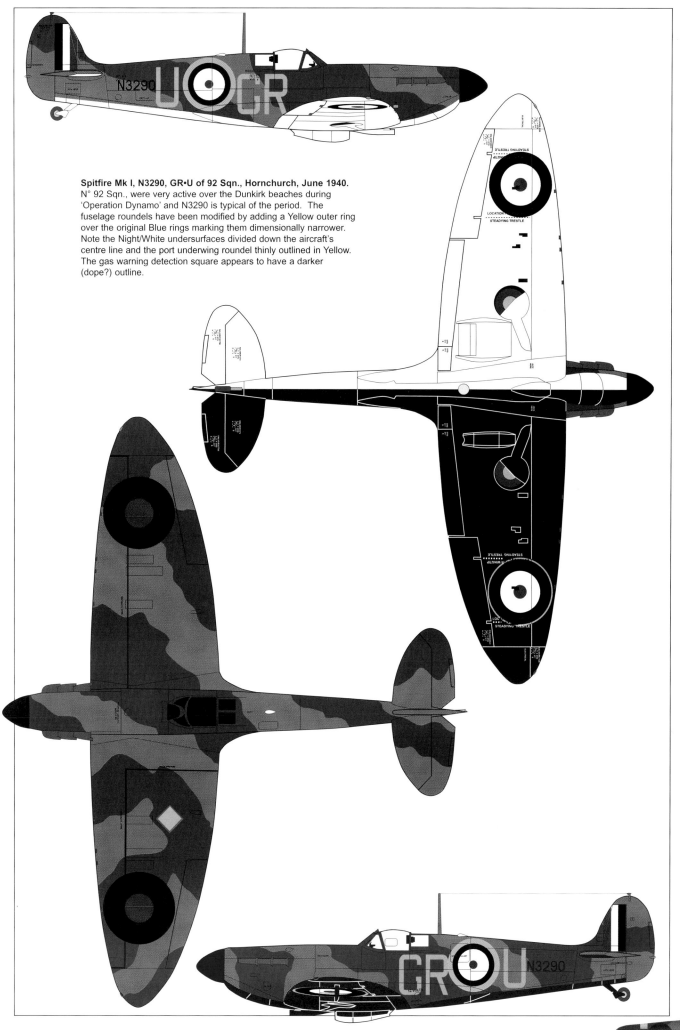

Spitfire Mk I, N3290, GR•U of 92 Sqn., Hornchurch, June 1940.
N° 92 Sqn., were very active over the Dunkirk beaches during
'Operation Dynamo' and N3290 is typical of the period. The
fuselage roundels have been modified by adding a Yellow outer ring
over the original Blue rings marking them dimensionally narrower.
Note the Night/White undersurfaces divided down the aircraft's
centre line and the port underwing roundel thinly outlined in Yellow.
The gas warning detection square appears to have a darker
(dope?) outline.

were L1576 - L1625, and delivery was expected to commence before the end of the month.

Once these aircraft began to go into service, during early April, Fighter Command expressed a wish that all Spitfires and Hurricanes should be finished in this manner. At this point, the matter seems to have come to the attention of the Director of Operations and Intelligence who expressed a wish that Fighter Command would reconsider their request that all Spitfire and Hurricane aircraft be finished in this way because it was felt that if friendly fighters were finished in this way during peacetime, a prospective enemy would learn of the marking and paint his own aircraft in the same way and thus defeat the object of having the defending fighters painted in this way.

Whilst Fighter Command briefly replied to this letter on 14 April, it was not until 10 June that Dowding himself wrote to the Air Ministry to make his position on this, and a number of other matters which had arisen in his absence, as clear as possible. Dowding thought that the idea that an enemy would copy the markings of British aircraft was "rather exploded" as the copying of markings had been constantly suggested during the Great War but had hardly ever happened. Dowding felt that the fact was that aircraft which imitated enemy markings were apt to receive more

undesirable attention from their own side over their own territory, than they would have from the enemy if they had retained their own markings.

On the subject of the black and white markings, Dowding complained that the Hurricanes which had been delivered by that time had not been properly painted, as he wished the black and white colours to cover the largest possible surface and to meet on the centreline. The Hurricanes supplied thus far had not been painted on the fuselage at all, leaving a 'silver' band between the black and white which caused the colours to blend into one another when seen from a distance, destroying the contrast.

He then went on to suggest that the National markings on the underside of Home Defence fighter aircraft were no longer necessary, as the black and white finish would act as sufficient identification from below and the National markings only served to break up the clean expanse of black and white which was being relied upon for recognition.

This latter suggestion was considered by the Air Ministry which concluded that there was no legal reason why this could not be done and, on 30 August 1938, the Director of Operations and Intelligence wrote to Fighter Command to inform them of the decision. It was however stated that the National markings must continue to be used in the 'Field Force' fighter

squadrons.

With September 1938, came the Munich crisis, and on 23 September, Fighter Command wrote to the Air Ministry to obtain permission to paint the undersides of the mainplanes of all fighters, with the exception of 'Field Force' fighters, black and white up to the centre line of the aircraft. This appears to have been granted as the black and white scheme spread very quickly amongst the Home Defence squadrons.

There were two notable features of this widespread adoption of the black and white scheme. The first was that it was applied to the undersides of both the upper and lower mainplanes of biplanes, and that on both the biplane types and the Hurricanes, the ailerons were often left in their Aluminium finish. This was due to the concern raised by the prospect of the application of the black or white paint to the ailerons upsetting their balance. Where Hurricane ailerons were repainted at a squadron level, no adverse effects were immediately apparent, but it was felt by the RAE, who were called in to investigate the matter, that even so, the safety margin built-in to the balance of these control surfaces must have been reduced. The RAE urged that the service should not paint the ailerons at all, but if they insisted on doing so, then the same procedure as for repaired ailerons should be adopted, with careful re-balancing being carried out. This meant that

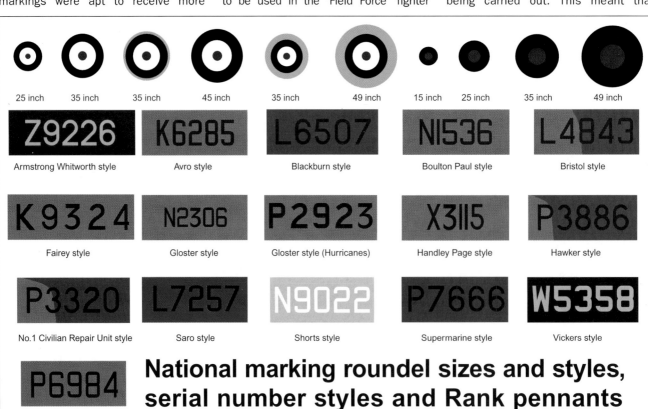

National marking roundel sizes and styles, serial number styles and Rank pennants

repainting the ailerons would not be a simple matter of quickly applying a couple of coats of paint.

Fighter Command however was adamant that the whole of the wing under surfaces including the ailerons should be finished in the black and white scheme, and on 25 November 1938, wrote to the Air Ministry to suggest that the ailerons should be finished in the appropriate colour on the production line, therefore avoiding the problem of over-balancing altogether. This of course implied that the black and white scheme would be applied to all new fighter aircraft on the production line.

At the conference held at the Air Ministry on 20 December 1938 to discuss the question of aircraft markings, it was agreed to accept the introduction of black and white markings on fighter aircraft during peacetime, and on 12 January, the Air Ministry wrote to Fighter Command to advise them that the aircraft contractors were to be advised that they should finish the ailerons of new production fighters in the black and white scheme. The letters doing this were sent to the RTOs at Hawkers and Supermarines on 27 January 1939.

The letters informed the RTOs that the decision had been made that fighter aircraft were to have the undersides of their wings painted, one wing black, the other white with the division between the colours running down the centreline of the aircraft. Even when this had been done, there was still considerable delay before aircraft began to leave the production lines in the new markings. At Supermarines for example, it was sometime around April 1939 before Spitfires began to leave the production line with the black and white under

An example of the Night/White undersurface scheme, divided centrally down the centreline, on Spitfire Mk I, RN·N (serial not known) of 72 Sqn., circa May/June 1940. Note the hard-edged uppersurface colours demarcation, painted-out serial number, exhaust glare shields infront of the windscreen - fitted for night flying exercises - and the 'pole type' TR 9 radio mast. The 'Kiwi'(?) badge under the glare shield is interesting.

surface markings.

This left the problem of those aircraft already delivered to the service which had originally been finished with their under surfaces in Aluminium, as called for in AD 1160. The wings of these aircraft, (but not their ailerons), had been repainted in Service. By 11 April, it appears to have been decided that as the silver ailerons did not appear to detract greatly from the black and white scheme, their continued use would have to be accepted for the time being. Arrangements were to be made to paint spare ailerons held in store in the correct colours so that they would gradually replace the incorrectly finished ones in units. Ultimately it was decided that the painting of the under surfaces of the ailerons would be undertaken by the manufacturers at their service depots.

The change in policy from fighters in peacetime having silver undersides to having black and white undersides was made following a conference held at the Air Ministry on 20 December 1938 to discuss the question of aircraft markings, and the decisions were promulgated in AMO A.154 in AMO A.154 - 'Identification Markings on Aircraft of Operational Units and Marking of Unit Equipment' dated 27 April 1939. The AMO stated that, "Fighter aircraft were not to carry the national marking on the lower surface of the wing tips, but the lower surface of the starboard mainplane and half the undersurface of the fuselage was to be painted white. The corresponding port side was to be painted black".

The exception to this rule was made for fighter aircraft stationed in France in AMO A.520 dated 7 December 1939, which stated that, "fighter aircraft stationed in France were to carry red, white and blue roundels".

It must be pointed out that although all the contemporary references to this scheme refer to it as being 'black and white', the colours actually applied to the aircraft appear to have been Night and White, the then standard identification colours.

This AMO set out the identification markings which were to be applied to all

British military aircraft in all roles in the light of experience gained during the first three months of the war. These markings were broken up into four categories, National Markings; Code Letters to indicate squadrons and the identity of individual aircraft within the squadron; Squadron Badges; and the Aircraft Number.

National marking (i) was defined as a blue ring surrounding a red centre, and was to be located on both sides of the fuselage and on the upper surfaces of the wing tips. National marking (ii) was defined as a blue ring surrounding a white ring with the latter surrounding a red centre, and was to be found on the lower surface of the wing tips.

The Code letters were defined as being two letters to indicate the squadron and one letter to indicate the individual aircraft, (as previously detailed).

The Squadron badge was to be that approved by HM The King and was to be located as laid down in Air Ministry Orders. Such badges were to be removable at short notice without leaving any trace.

The Aircraft number was defined as the Air Ministry letter and number allocated to the aircraft, (serial number), and was to be located underneath the lower mainplanes and at the rear end of the fuselage.

Rank Pennants

One marking not apparently considered in any of the foregoing deliberations were the Officers' Rank Pennants which were often applied to aircraft flown by officers of Squadron Leader rank and above. Heraldically, such markings are probably related to the pennants flown by Knights from their lances as they went into battle. In the RAF, the tradition had started during the 1914-18 war when Flight and Squadron commanders flew coloured streamers from the struts of their biplanes for identification purposes. With the advent of the high speed metal monoplane from the mid 1930s onward, it became the practice to paint pennant flags on the fuselages of aircraft, usually beneath the cockpit area, a practice which continues to the present day.

CHAPTER 3
SHADES OF SKY

November 1936 - April 1940

Development of a camouflage finish for the under surface of day flying aircraft began in 1936 as a follow-on from work done on the sea camouflage scheme. On 24 November, the Air Ministry wrote to the RAE in connection with the sea scheme trials to say that whilst the proposed colours for the upper surfaces appeared to be suitable, no investigation of colour for the lower surface appears to have been carried out. The Admiralty had suggested that the whole of the lower surfaces and the vertical parts of the airframe, such as the fin and rudder, should be painted in one colour, ideally a 'dirty white' or a paler version of 'marking grey'. This was because the Admiralty considered that the camouflage of Fleet Air Arm aircraft should be designed to reduce visibility at long range against a uniform background, and held the view that such invisibility would best be achieved with a matt finish, and by painting the lower surfaces a uniform colour to tone with the clouds and sky, whilst the upper surfaces were to tone with the sea. Invisibility against a cloud background was considered to be of chief importance.

The RAE was asked to prepare a

quantity of some suitable camouflage colours, which, when dispatched from the RAE on 21 December 1936, included 10 gallons of a colour called Sky Grey. Trials with this colour were successful and Sky Grey was adopted as the standard under

surface camouflage colour for Fleet Air Arm aircraft.

Work on a suitable camouflage colour for the undersides of day flying aircraft for the rest of the RAF seems to have been given a much lower priority, the RAE not

Heading: Blenheim IV, V6240, YH·B of 21 Sqn., circa June 1940, showing the production demarcation line between the Temperate Land Scheme uppersurfaces and the then new Sky undersurfaces.

Right: Blenheims repainted in Service hands very often had an irregular wavy demarcation line between the upper and under surface colours. This Mk IV bomber, L8756, XD·E of 139 Sqn., circa May/June 1940, (top) shows a straight demarcation on the forward fuselage and wavy demarcation on the rear fuselage. Note that whilst the fin stripes have been added, the fuselage roundel is still without the yellow outline. The line-up of 82 Squadron's Mk IVs, (opposite) shows a variety of styles. Unfortunately, it is impossible to tell what colour has been used on the undersurfaces! Identifiable aircraft are P6915, UX·A and P6628, UK·K.

The 'light' undersurface colour applied to both Blenheim Day Bombers and Day Fighters, such as this Mk IVf Z6029, QY•L of 254 Sqn., is difficult to accurately assess, and may always be open to interpretation.

being asked to put any tests in hand to determine a suitable scheme until 18 March 1938. Even when this had been done, the work does not seem to have proceeded at any great pace as the report on the RAE's findings was not tendered to the Air Ministry until March of 1939, by which time it had been concluded that matt white offered the best scheme for day bombers. Despite this finding, nothing further seems to have been done about adopting white undersurface camouflage at this time.

Sky Blue came about as the result of an Air Ministry letter to the RAE dated 7 February 1939, requesting that three Air Diagrams be prepared. Amongst these was Air Diagram 1171 which was to be entitled 'Camouflage Scheme for Target Aircraft', and was to be suitable for de Havilland Queen Wasp target aircraft. The Air Ministry specified that the colour scheme should show all the under surfaces of the main and tail planes, fuselage and vertical sides of the fuselage in a colour referred to as 'sky-blue' with the upper surfaces in 'yellow'.

The original letter has a handwritten asterisk next to 'sky-blue' and the same hand has added a note underneath the text of the letter stating, "as near as possible to the German colour". This suggests that the intention was possibly to make the undersurfaces look as much like a German aircraft as possible. The Air Diagram was prepared and submitted to the Air Ministry on 27 February 1939, showing Sky Blue as a camouflage colour. As far as is known, this scheme was never applied to any Queen Wasp aircraft as, by the time the type finally entered service, the camouflage requirements for target aircraft had changed.

By July 1939, some concern was being felt at Bomber Command about the undersurface colouring of its aircraft. The Night undersurfaces were felt to make them conspicuous by day against a sky background, and it was by day that most of the flying over enemy territory was envisaged as being carried out. It therefore seemed that all bombers not definitely allocated to night operations should be painted a colour, or combination of colours, which would make them as inconspicuous as possible against various forms of sky background. If any of these aircraft were required for operations at night, it was thought that the undersurfaces could easily be blacked over with a temporary matt finish. It was also thought that a suitable undersurface colour might be silver, light blue, or grey, or some other colour or

This Blenheim IV, thought to be L9241, of 110 Sqn., shot down over Poix in May 1940, was originally painted Night on its undersurfaces but has been repainted in service in an unidentifiable 'light colour'. (via Michael Payne)

combination of colours.

Despite these feelings of unease by Bomber Command, no further work on camouflage finishes for the under surfaces of day flying aircraft seems to have been done, until the outbreak of war in September brought the activities of Sidney Cotton and the Photographic Development Unit at Heston to the attention of higher authority.

This unit had been set up as a result of a meeting held at the Air Ministry on 22 March 1939, where it was decided to form an experimental unit for the purpose of testing, and if successful, developing, what were then considered novel techniques for making photo reconnaissance sorties over enemy territory. The basis of the scheme proposed was the use of high speed and invisibility, and the originator of the scheme, F S Cotton was put in charge.

The unit's initial equipment was the Bristol Blenheim which was soon found to be too slow and, with Night under surfaces, too visible from below. The cure for the first problem was to make a determined attempt to clean-up the airframe as much as possible, and the cure for the second problem was to apply a different, lighter, colour to the undersurfaces.

It has been claimed that prior to the war, Sidney Cotton was involved in carrying out clandestine photography whilst engaged on what were ostensibly legitimate flights over Germany on behalf of the Secret Intelligence Service. The aircraft he used on these flights are said to have been painted a 'very pale green colour' which did not look out of place on a civil aircraft, but at the same time

happened to be very good at concealing the aircraft from observers on the ground. It would appear that it was this 'very pale green colour' which was applied to the undersurfaces of the Blenheims at Heston.

Bomber Command evidently heard something of the PDUs work on modifying the Blenheim as, during October, a Blenheim from No 139 Sqn was sent to Heston to be modified in a similar manner to the Blenheims of the PDU. As part of these modifications, the aircraft received the glossy camouflage paints then in use at Heston, consisting of the normal Dark Earth and Dark Green colours applied in the usual disruptive pattern on the upper surfaces, and what was apparently described as a 'light sea green' colour on the under surfaces.

This new camouflage seems to have been reported in some detail to the Air Ministry as, during early November, the Air Ministry expressed a wish for representatives of the RAE to pay the PDU at Heston a visit and give the Air Ministry their opinion as to the advantages and disadvantages of the PDU's camouflage scheme. As a result, two representatives from the RAE travelled to Heston on 18 November 1939.

They found that a Blenheim Mk IV had been extensively worked upon to eliminate gaps in the skin joints and had been given a very smooth, glossy, paint finish with the usual Dark Green and Dark Earth disruptive pattern on the upper surfaces and a colour described in the subsequent RAE report as "Duck Egg Green termed Camotint" on its undersurfaces. It was claimed that this

'Duck Egg Green' finish rendered the aircraft practically invisible at heights of 10,000ft and upwards.

Whilst it had been found that the new smooth finish had helped to improve the performance of the Blenheim, it had been realised that the glossiness would compromise the camouflage effect. It was therefore requested that the RAE supply Heston with a suitable paint which would match the Dark Earth, Dark Green and Duck Egg Green in colour and would be smoother than the standard camouflage finishes but without the glossiness of the dopes currently being used.

Bomber Command meanwhile, was apparently most impressed with its 'streamlined' Blenheim on 139 Sqn as, on 25 November 1939, HQ Bomber Command wrote to both the Air Ministry and HQ Fighter Command, to inform them that experiments had been carried out at Watton on Blenheims of 139 Sqn to 'clean-up' the aircraft with a view to increasing their speed. At that time, the experiments had been judged a successes and it was intended to continue the work on other Blenheim squadrons in the Command.

The letter then went on to state that

Spitfire Mk I, N3093, QJ·W of 616 Sqn., circa June/July 1940, with its undersurfaces repainted in what the pilot termed "a pale blue" - but was this Air Ministry Sky Blue, BSS 381 (1930) Sky Blue, or a Squadron mixed paint!?!

coincident with this process a change had been made in the undersurface colour of these Blenheims which were now painted what was described as 'Grey-Blue' so as to merge into the background of the sky when viewed from below. Bomber Command wished that this change of colouring should be brought to the attention of all concerned as the change was being progressively introduced into Blenheim bomber squadrons; and it would also be necessary to inform the French authorities as two of these squadrons of repainted Blenheims were to replace two Fairey Battle squadrons in France in the very near future.

Accordingly, on 29 November 1939, signals A399 and A432 informed No 1 Mission for onward transmission to the French, and all home based forces respectively, that a 'Light Blue' colour was being introduced for the under surfaces of Blenheim bombers instead of the present black finish. The Air Ministry informed Bomber Command that this had been done in a letter dated 2 December 1939. The letter also informed Bomber Command that the Air Ministry approved of the change in colouring and that red, white and blue roundels were to be carried on the undersurfaces of the wings of aircraft painted in the 'blue-grey' colour scheme.

It is not clear exactly what this colour, described in the official correspondence

Left upper: A tantalising glimpse of the undersurface colour on the wing tip of Spitfire Mk I, N3249, QJ·P of 92 Sqn., which could be a duck egg blue shade, whilst Hurricane V6825, TM·F of 504 Sqn., (opposite) may have the duck egg green BS 381 (1930) Eau-de-Nil shade, or perhaps even standard Sky. Note the pointed Rotol spinner which was just being introduced.

seen by the author merely as 'blue-grey' and 'light blue', actually was. Available photographic evidence suggests that it was much lighter than Medium Sea Grey, and in this author's opinion, it was most likely Air Ministry Sky Blue. However, archaeological evidence suggests that there might have been a blue grey colour in use at about this time. A 'Light Blue-Grey' colour was found on the remains of Hurricane P2728 at Hawkinge which has already been mentioned in the previous Chapter in connection with the colour of the pre-war code letters. Photographs 3 and 4, on this book's inside front cover, show a panel from the under surface of one of the wings of this aircraft.

By mid-December, the Air Ministry was trying to get such improvements as it could, incorporated into Blenheims on the production line. There were however, apparently problems with the camouflage finish. On 10 January 1940, a meeting was held in the Air Ministry to try to get to grips with the problems thrown up by the introduction of two new under surface camouflage materials, one of which was Camotint.

The first problem which had arisen with Camotint had been the means by which it was obtained. Heston seems to have been in the habit of obtaining its materials direct from the manufacturer, Titanine. Therefore, when Bomber Command began submitting demands for this same material to the Air Ministry for use on its day flying Blenheims, nothing was known about it by the Directorate of Engineering. Not being able to obtain supplies of this material might have been the reason why Bomber Command used the light blue colour instead.

It was suggested that a technical leaflet might be published giving full instructions regarding the various materials used to obtain the new finish, together with the method of their application, and that an AMO be issued introducing the items for use on all Blenheims. In this connection it was stated that the question of re-painting Blenheim Fighter squadrons was under consideration.

The overriding concern at that moment however was one of provisioning the new colour. The initial problem was

that it needed to be determined exactly what quantities of this new material were required for maintainance purposes on such aircraft as were already finished in Camotint, and for repainting Blenheims held by the Aircraft Storage Units awaiting issue. In the longer term, should the new finish be approved for general use, some estimate of the amount of material which would be required was needed. At that time samples of Camotint were being prepared by Cellon as an alternative supply to Titanine, but no difficulties were envisaged in obtaining supplies of the new materials from any of the approved paint manufacturers

Whilst all of this had been going on, work had been put in hand at the RAE to produce a finish employing a very finely ground pigment which it was hoped would give a smooth matt finish. On 25 January 1940, the RAE despatched to Heston, 5 gallons of Dark Green Type S, 5 gallons of Dark Earth Type S, and 20 gallons of Sky Type S.

Sky was the name given by the RAE to the 'duck egg green' colour known at Heston as Camotint.

The suffix 'Type S' was the name given by the RAE to the new smooth paint which featured a more finely ground pigment which resulted in a smaller particle size and thus a smoother finish. This new material will be examined in more detail in a later chapter.

Thus, by the end of January 1940, the only Sky 'Type S' available was in the hands of the PDU at Heston, having been supplied in very small quantities by the RAE. In February however, Bristols appear to have modified the camouflage scheme of the Blenheims they were producing to have what has been described as 'light green' undersurfaces. This is understood to have been the first use of Sky on a production aircraft, but this was almost certainly not to the new 'Type S' standard; more than likely being the same material that Titanine had been supplying to the PDU which appears to have been a gloss finish to DTD specification DTD 63A.

An eyewitness account suggests that Blenheims built by The Bristol Aeroplane Company at Filton during the early part of 1940, were finished in the correct colour

Sky, even though the materials used were probably not Type S.

Supporting evidence for this is a letter dated 20 April 1940, sent by the Air Ministry to Bristols headed "Camotint - Specification for". In it, Bristols were told that, "It is agreed that you should call on the schedule for Mod 864 on the Blenheim IV for Lacquer to DTD 63 with reduced gloss. The gloss is not to exceed that shown on samples to be obtained from the Bristol Aeroplane Co Ltd. This degree of gloss is to be permitted on the Blenheim IV only, all other aircraft will comply with the new 'Type S' standard. You will arrange with Rootes to supply samples finished with the above DTD 63 with reduced gloss. As regards colour, the pale blue-green which has been called Camotint is now defined as Standard Sky and this description should be given in your schedule".

DTD 63A was a then current aircraft finish specification listed in Aircraft Design Memorandum 332, 'External Finish of Aircraft (issue 2)' dated 8 September 1939. DTD 63A was a Material Specification for Cellulose Enamels and Primers for use on metal or timber which was apparently available in a whole range of colours, including those of the Air Ministry - for example, Dark Green and Dark Earth. It was to be suitable for application by brush or spray and originally was to dry to a uniformly smooth covering having a glossy finish. However, in an amendment dated March 1940, the requirement for the material to dry to a glossy finish was dropped, presumably leading to the finish which the Air Ministry referred to as 'DTD 63A with reduced gloss' from April onwards.

CHAPTER 4 'TYPE S'

November 1939 - April 1940

The second innovation in British aircraft camouflage to come about as a result of the RAE visit to Heston in November 1939, was the advent of the new 'Type S' paint. Right from the introduction of camouflage paints in 1937, there had been some debate about the effect on aerodynamic smoothness of the introduction of the camouflage finish. Particular reference had been made to the Fairey Battle having its performance impared by the application of the paint. Investigation of this matter by the RAE had revealed that the rough surface finish being obtained on the Battle was not due to the paint itself, but by its 'inept application' by the manufacturer in less than ideal circumstances. Once the RAE's findings became known, the debate seems to have died down.

It would appear that Sidney Cotton's inclusion of a smooth gloss finish in the cleaning-up process carried out on the Blenheim, re-opened the debate early in 1940. Even whilst the RAE was in the process of producing the initial quantity of smooth camouflage paint for the PDU, moves began to be made to try and improve the surface finish of Service aircraft. On 9 January 1940, a note was produced at Farnborough entitled 'Possible methods of obtaining smoother

finish on Production Aircraft'. This note opened by stating that the cleaning-up, which was being put in hand on numerous types of aircraft on the production line, called for a surface smoothness on certain parts of the aircraft such that the roughness height did not exceed one half of one thou of an inch.

There were considered to be three alternatives which were open to the aircraft manufacturers to achieve this result.

Firstly, they could use different paint materials which were easier to apply and were not liable to dry with an excessive roughness due to unskilled spraying, especially where colours overlapped.

Secondly, the existing paint materials and methods of application could be retained, and the final finish could be rubbed down lightly by applying Wet and Dry paper used wet. If this method was used, then care would have to be taken to avoid rubbing rivet heads and other proud edges bare.

Thirdly, the existing paint materials could be retained but the method of

application could be greatly revised by exercising careful control over the humidity and temperature of the paint shops; avoiding drafts and air movements in the paint shop; avoiding dust on the floors and in the air; ensuring more careful use of the spraying equipment to avoid partially dry or dry spray particles; abolishing the merging of adjacent colours at the pattern outlines; preparing a smooth undercoat by rubbing down with abrasives before application of the finishing coat; and finally avoiding long storage of the paint before it was used.

This final alternative was considered to be a non-starter as it might involve the manufacturers in serious changes in the layout of their dope rooms and prove impractical. There therefore remained the first and second alternatives, and the choice of which one to adopt would appear to lie with the aircraft manufacturers. Both paint and aircraft manufacturers would shortly receive samples of the finish now required and be acceptable from the point of view of gloss.

Heading: A pair of Spitfires of 41 Sqn., (EB·N, serial number unreadable, and X4178, EB·K), photographed circa September 1940, showing a distinct sheen which may well be indicative of the use of Type S camouflage paints. Undersurfaces are thought to have been in Sky Grey!

Right: From February 1940 onwards, the Bristol Aeroplane Co at Filton, were finishing their Blenheims in camouflage colours to 'DTD 63A with reduced gloss'. This resulted in quite a shiny surface illustrated by N3537, TR·J of 59 Sqn.

Boulton Paul were visited by representatives of the RAE in February 1940 to discuss the problems with applying a smoother paint finish to their Defiant aircraft. This particular machine, possibly on a test flight, appears to have slightly glossy light coloured undersurfaces, which may be BSS 381 (1930) Eau-de-Nil to DTD 63A with reduced gloss.

Over the next few months, representatives from the RAE visited a number of aircraft companies to inspect the current standards of finish, and to discuss improvements with these aircraft manufacturers. Fairly typical of these visits was the one made on 20 February to Boulton Paul at Wolverhampton, to discuss the production of a smoother finish on Defiant aircraft.

Several completed airframes were inspected and the roughness of the colour bands on the wings was found to be of the order of one to three mils, but at the edges where the colours were blended the roughness was much greater, being up to ten mils. Painting was being carried out in a heated shed which was sectioned off with heavy curtains to reduce draughts, but there was found to be a considerable amount of dust on the concrete floor. No spraying was in progress at the time of the visit.

Methods of improving the finish were discussed with the manufacturers, but the suggested method of rubbing down the final coat with Wet and Dry sandpaper was considered to involve a large increase in the time necessary to camouflage an aircraft. Boulton Paul did not raise any objection to the idea of removing the blending of the colours by using masks to protect the already finished surface from the particles which caused surface roughness, but they requested written authority for them to do this as their present instructions called for the colour boundaries to be blended. With regard to the final finish, the manufacturer expressed a preference to use a paint with a more finely ground pigment than to rub down the present material.

On 15 March 1940, a meeting was held to review the present position relating to the introduction of 'Smooth Paint Finish on Aircraft' and to consider the effect that this change would make on production, maintenance, aircraft speed and camouflage. It was pointed out that this question was part of the general problem of improving the aerodynamic cleanness of Service aircraft on which work was actively proceeding. The surface finish which was required was one of aerodynamic smoothness and not gloss.

The discussion was taken under the four headings already mentioned, ie the effect on the projected change on production (and inspection); maintenance; improvement in aircraft

speed; and camouflage, ie the possibility that the new finish would increase the visibility of the aircraft.

Effect on production
It was thought that production would be adversely affected if the process time for the painting operation was increased. Application of the new Type S paint was exactly the same as that of the existing matt paints, the only difference between the two being the reduced grain size of the pigment in the Type S paint. Unless strict precautions were observed in the paint room, particularly with regard to the avoidance of dust, it was preferable to rub down the undercoat before applying the Type S finish. A similar result could be obtained by a final rubbing down of the existing matt paint.

Experiments had been made by rubbing down a Spitfire wing which showed that it might take as much as 10 man hours to rub down the whole machine when washing and drying time were taken into account. Such an increase in the process time would necessitate an increase in floor space and the provision of the necessary facilities which might not be practicable at some factories. It was also felt that the class of labour which would be employed on this work could not be relied on to avoid rubbing all the paint off protuberences such as rivet heads!

It was stated that without rubbing down or special precautions, better results would be expected by using the

new Type S paint. Further to this, improvement was possible by avoiding excessive roughness at the merging of colours on the boundaries of the camouflage colours. It was agreed that this could be brought about by a simple change in the painting process by using masks to get a hard edge to the camouflage pattern and by making the gradual merging of colours no longer obligatory. It was thought that this change in technique would not appreciably increase the process time for painting.

The meeting agreed that the new Type S paint could be adopted to advantage without affecting production, and it would be left to individual aircraft manufacturers to produce the desired smoothness, either by greater care in spraying or by rubbing down the final finish. It was also agreed that it would be impracticable to impose rigid inspection methods to ensure that the required surface finish was obtained. It was suggested that a large panel showing the required finish could be displayed in the paint room.

The effect on Maintenance and Inspection
No effect on maintenance was foreseen. It was thought however that it might be necessary for the Service and contractors involved in the assembly process to take increased precautions to avoid damaging the finished surface. Individual units

The original camouflage paints to DTD 308 and DTD 314 gave a matt finish illustrated by this Hurricane of 145 Sqn. Note the non-standard canopy with teardrop side panels!

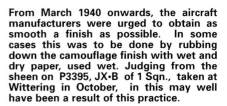

From March 1940 onwards, the aircraft manufacturers were urged to obtain as smooth a finish as possible. In some cases this was to be done by rubbing down the camouflage finish with wet and dry paper, used wet. Judging from the sheen on P3395, JX·B of 1 Sqn., taken at Wittering in October, in this may well have been a result of this practice.

would be left to use their own discretion in deciding how much rubbing down was necessary in making good surface defects. This in turn would depend upon the degree of urgency involved in getting the job finished, although it would of course be preferable to encourage the aircraft manufacturers to meet the requirements.

Improvements in aircraft speed
It was stated that an improvement in the speed of a Blenheim of between 2 -5 mph was to be expected from using a smoother surface finish and approximately the same result was obtained on the Hampden. It was felt that this increase in speed was well worth striving for.

Effect on camouflage
It was stated that the surface obtained with the new Type S paint had a greater reflecting power than the matt surface then in use. It was difficult to assess the reflecting power precisely in terms of increased visibility in the air or on the ground, although it was noted that a much shinier surface had been accepted for Blenheim bomber aircraft.

It was agreed by the meeting that the improvement in speed appeared to to justify this slight reduction in camouflage effect, but this was a matter for the Air Staff to decide, as was the question as to which types of aircraft were to be so treated. The meeting was of the opinion

that such types as the Anson and Battle should not have any special effort made to improve their surface finish.

Retrospective action
Retrospective action on aircraft already in service was not contemplated, and the change to Type S finish would be introduced on the production line as soon as possible if the recommendations of the meeting were accepted by the Air Staff. Existing stocks of paint would be used up first.

Recommendations
The meeting made the following recommendations to the Air Staff.
1) Type S paint for camouflage finish was to be introduced in production as soon as possible, subject to the acceptance by the Air Staff of the departure from the matt finish then in use.
2) No retrospective action on aircraft already in service was to be taken and existing stocks of matt paint were to be used up.
3) Aircraft manufacturers were to be asked to improve the surface finish as much as possible, taking the new standard as showing the maximum amount of gloss allowable. The maximum roughness of one thousandth of one inch was to be aimed at. Rigid inspectional control would not be possible, so the local technical committees were to explain to the firms the need for this finish and encourage them to achieve the

required results.
4) No change in the specification of the paint was thought necessary. The new paint was specified to the existing Specification Number (Type S). New standards were to be issued by RAE to the paint and aircraft manufacturers.

The recommendations were approved by the Air Staff, and in late April a circular was sent to all RTOs entitled 'Improving Surface finish of aircraft; adoption of Type S paints'.

The letter opened by reminding RTOs that their attention had already been drawn to the necessity of producing a smooth finish on production aircraft, something of the order of less than one thousandth of an inch, but that it should be noted that the final roughness on many aircraft types was often as high as five thousandths of an inch and sometimes up to ten thousandths of an inch. RTOs were informed that in order to assist still further towards achieving the desired result, it had now been agreed that the camouflage paints themselves were to be altered so that they were easier to apply and not so liable to give a rough finish due to unskilled application. The change in the manufacture of the paints was one of finer grinding of the pigment, so reducing the pigment size. It was to be noted that this would not prevent the paints from still being liable to coagulate into lumps if they were not used whilst still fresh. No change would be made to the specification number, but the words 'Type S' would be added to the title.

New Standards, ie sample panels, would be issued to the aircraft firms by the RAE. These Standards would show the maximum permissible gloss and indicate the degree of smoothness towards which the firm should strive. If the firm was to experience any difficulty in producing finishes which met the new Standards, they were to seek help immediately from their paint supplier. All the firms involved in the manufacture of paints and dopes were fully aware of the new requirements.

It was stressed that it was most important that the final gloss on the finished surface should not exceed that of the Standards as otherwise the efficiency of the camouflage would be reduced. To assist in avoiding dry or partially dry spraying at the colour boundaries, it had now been agreed that colour merging need not be done. Instead

Note the sheen on the paintwork of these two Spitfires of 616 Sqn., QJ·Y and QJ·R, taxiing for take-off into an almost cloudless summer sky, (probably in August). Unfortunately the serial numbers are unreadable.

Variations in Day Fighter undersurface finishes - May to December 1940

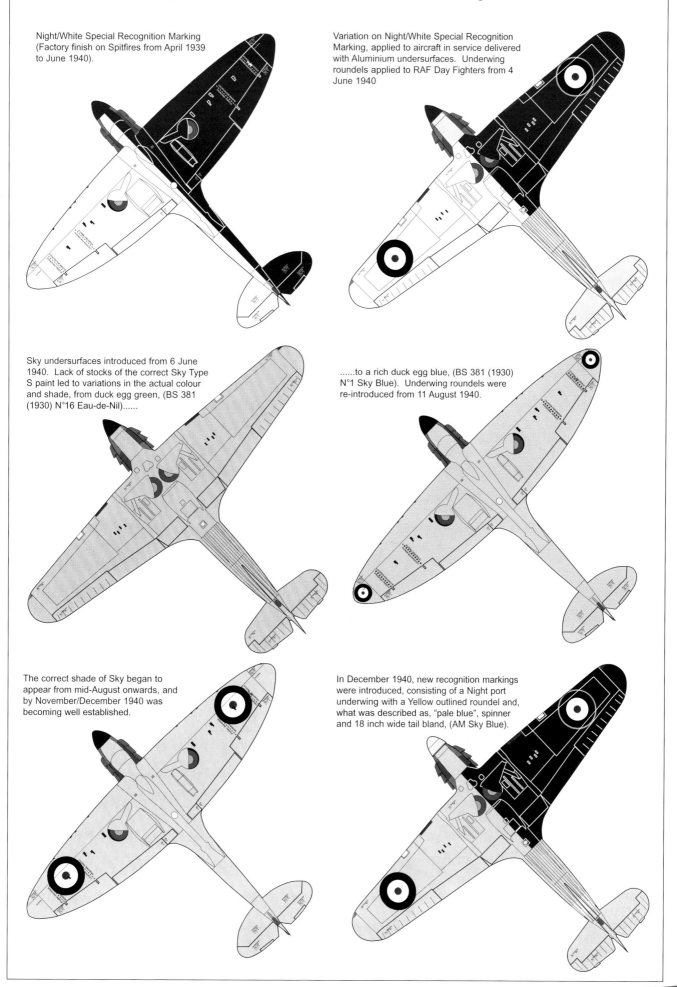

Night/White Special Recognition Marking (Factory finish on Spitfires from April 1939 to June 1940).

Variation on Night/White Special Recognition Marking, applied to aircraft in service delivered with Aluminium undersurfaces. Underwing roundels applied to RAF Day Fighters from 4 June 1940

Sky undersurfaces introduced from 6 June 1940. Lack of stocks of the correct Sky Type S paint led to variations in the actual colour and shade, from duck egg green, (BS 381 (1930) N°16 Eau-de-Nil)......

......to a rich duck egg blue, (BS 381 (1930) N°1 Sky Blue). Underwing roundels were re-introduced from 11 August 1940.

The correct shade of Sky began to appear from mid-August onwards, and by November/December 1940 was becoming well established.

In December 1940, new recognition markings were introduced, consisting of a Night port underwing with a Yellow outlined roundel and, what was described as, "pale blue", spinner and 18 inch wide tail bland, (AM Sky Blue).

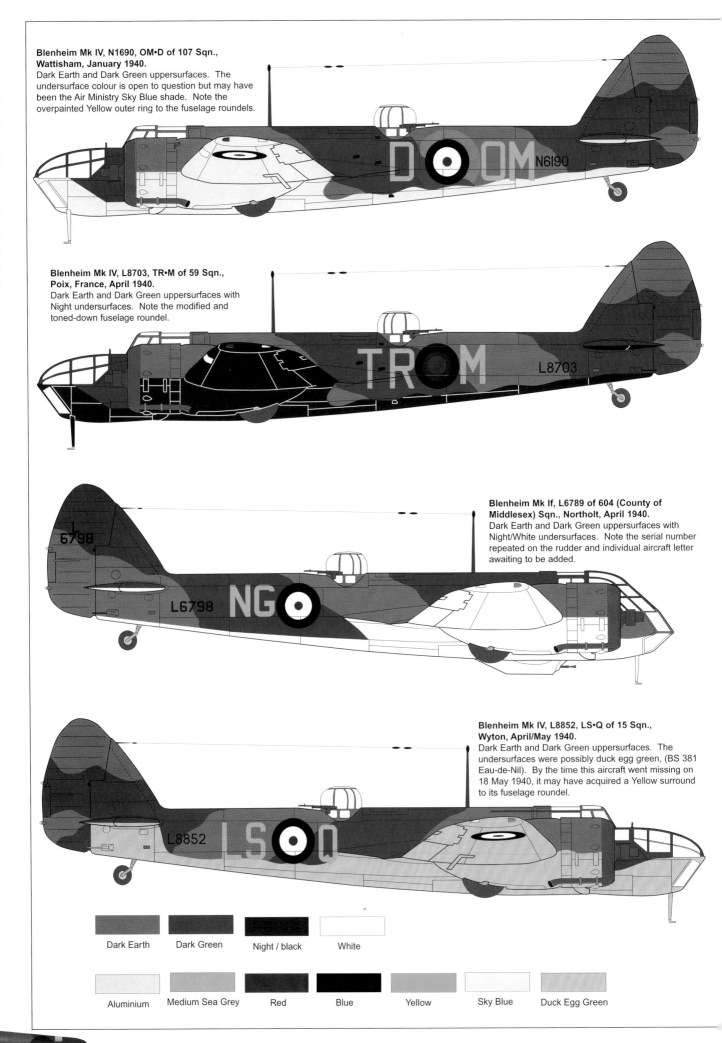

Blenheim Mk IV, N1690, OM•D of 107 Sqn., Wattisham, January 1940.
Dark Earth and Dark Green uppersurfaces. The undersurface colour is open to question but may have been the Air Ministry Sky Blue shade. Note the overpainted Yellow outer ring to the fuselage roundels.

Blenheim Mk IV, L8703, TR•M of 59 Sqn., Poix, France, April 1940.
Dark Earth and Dark Green uppersurfaces with Night undersurfaces. Note the modified and toned-down fuselage roundel.

Blenheim Mk If, L6789 of 604 (County of Middlesex) Sqn., Northolt, April 1940.
Dark Earth and Dark Green uppersurfaces with Night/White undersurfaces. Note the serial number repeated on the rudder and individual aircraft letter awaiting to be added.

Blenheim Mk IV, L8852, LS•Q of 15 Sqn., Wyton, April/May 1940.
Dark Earth and Dark Green uppersurfaces. The undersurfaces were possibly duck egg green, (BS 381 Eau-de-Nil). By the time this aircraft went missing on 18 May 1940, it may have acquired a Yellow surround to its fuselage roundel.

Dark Earth	Dark Green	Night / black	White

Aluminium	Medium Sea Grey	Red	Blue	Yellow	Sky Blue	Duck Egg Green

Spitfire Mk I, serial overpainted (?), RN•N of 72 Sqn., Gravesend, May 1940.
Dark Earth and Dark Green uppersurfaces with Night/White undersurfaces
divided equally down the fuselage centre line. Note the Yellow outline added to
the fuselage roundels and fin stripes.

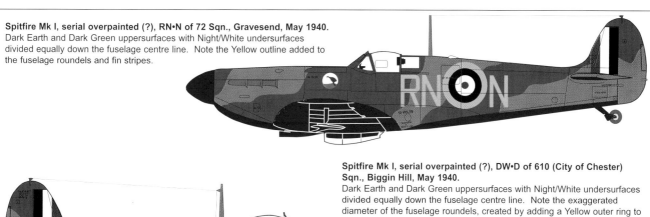

**Spitfire Mk I, serial overpainted (?), DW•D of 610 (City of Chester)
Sqn., Biggin Hill, May 1940.**
Dark Earth and Dark Green uppersurfaces with Night/White undersurfaces
divided equally down the fuselage centre line. Note the exaggerated
diameter of the fuselage roundels, created by adding a Yellow outer ring to
the original Red/White/Blue roundels.

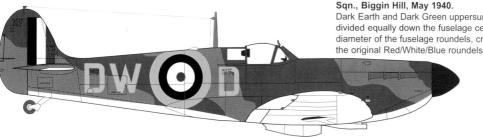

**Hurricane Mk I, P2617, AF•F of 607 (County of Durham) Sqn.,
Usworth, May 1940.**
Dark Earth and Dark Green uppersurfaces with Night/White/Aluminium
undersurfaces. Fin stripes, and the Yellow outer ring to fuselage roundels
have not yet been added, although underwing roundels are in evidence.
This is a typical example of the markings variations to be found amongst
RAF Squadron aircraft during this period.

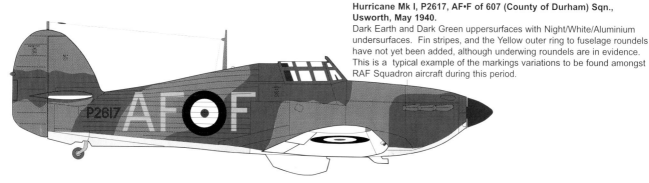

Hurricane Mk I, L1774, LK•D of 87 Sqn., Lille/Seclin, France, May 1940.
Dark Earth and Dark Green uppersurfaces with Night/White undersurfaces
divided equally down the fuselage centre line. Note the thin Yellow outline to
the fuselage roundels and the Watts two-blade wooden propeller. There
was no Yellow outline to the port underwing roundel.

Hurricane Mk I, L1754, DZ•E of 151 Sqn., Martlesham Heath, May/June 1940.
Dark Earth and Dark Green uppersurfaces with Night/White undersurfaces
divided equally down the fuselage centre line. Note the way the Yellow outer
ring, added to the original Red/White/Blue fuselage roundel, is terminated along
the upper/under surface camouflage demarcation line, and how the entire portion
of the front of the fin has been painted Red, with 9 inch wide stripes of White
and Blue. There was no Yellow outline to the port underwing roundel.

Hurricane Mk I, serial overpainted, SO•E of 145 Sqn., Croydon, early June 1940.
Dark Earth and Dark Green uppersurfaces with 'light coloured', (possibly duck egg
green?), undersurfaces. Note the narrow Yellow ring to the fuselage roundels,
and the fin stripes not extending up the full height of the fin.

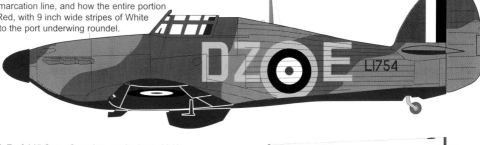

Hurricane Mk I, P2946, VK•A of 238 Sqn., Middle Wallop, July 1940.
Dark Earth and Dark Green uppersurfaces with duck egg blue/Sky Blue (?) undersurfaces. Note the Bright Red and Bright Blue shades of the fuselage roundel and broad, approx. 12 inch wide, Red, White, Blue fin stripes.

Note: All the undersurface colours are provisional, and based upon b&w photograph interpretation.

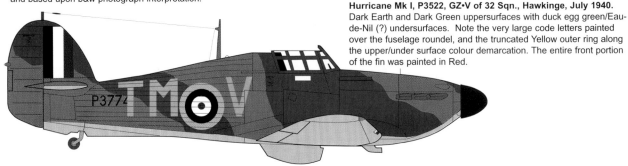

Hurricane Mk I, P3522, GZ•V of 32 Sqn., Hawkinge, July 1940.
Dark Earth and Dark Green uppersurfaces with duck egg green/Eau-de-Nil (?) undersurfaces. Note the very large code letters painted over the fuselage roundel, and the truncated Yellow outer ring along the upper/under surface colour demarcation. The entire front portion of the fin was painted in Red.

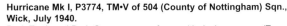

Hurricane Mk I, P3774, TM•V of 504 (County of Nottingham) Sqn., Wick, July 1940.
Dark Earth and Dark Green uppersurfaces with duck egg green/Eau-de-Nil (?) undersurfaces. Note the contrast in fuselage roundel size and fin stripe presentation to the aircraft above.

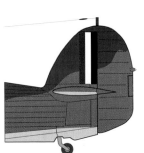

5 inch wide stripes on Hurricane (full height of fin)

6 inch wide stripes on Hurricane (full height of fin)

7 inch wide stripes on Hurricane (full height of fin)

7 inch (and/or 9 inch) wide White and Blue stripes with rest of fin in Red, only applied to Hurricanes.

24 inch wide x 27 inch high fin flash introduced in August 1940 (on Hurricane)

Fin Stripe Marking variations

7 inch wide stripes on Spitfire (full height of fin)

24 inch wide x 27 inch high fin flash introduced in August 1940 (on Spitfire)

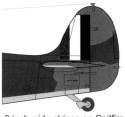

8 inch wide stripes on Spitfire variation (full height of fin)

Hurricane Mk I, P3144, GZ•B of 32 Sqn., Hawkinge, July 1940.
Dark Earth and Dark Green uppersurfaces with duck egg green/Eau-de-Nil (?) undersurfaces. Note the Bright Red and Bright Blue colours of the fuselage roundels, (and upperwing roundels), and the fin stripes found on many Gloster-built Hurricanes of this period.

Hurricane Mk I, N2572, US•P of 56 Sqn., North Weald, July 1940.
Dark Earth and Dark Green uppersurfaces with duck egg green/Eau-de-Nil (?) undersurfaces. Note the way the Yellow outer ring of the fuselage roundel has been painted around the code letters.

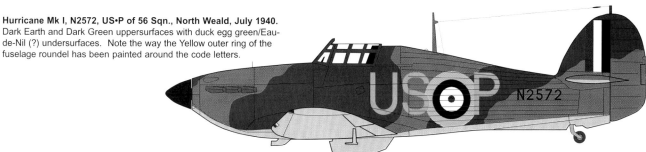

Spitfire Mk I, N3029, DW•K of 610 (City of Chester) Sqn., Biggin Hill, July 1940.
Dark Earth and Dark Green uppersurfaces with duck egg blue/Sky Blue (?) undersurfaces. Note that the serial number may have been painted out on this machine.

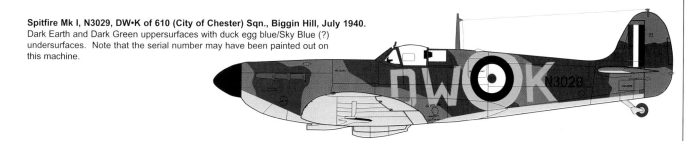

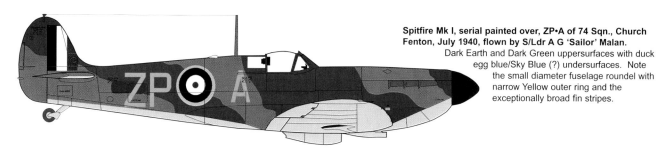

Spitfire Mk I, serial painted over, ZP•A of 74 Sqn., Church Fenton, July 1940, flown by S/Ldr A G 'Sailor' Malan.
Dark Earth and Dark Green uppersurfaces with duck egg blue/Sky Blue (?) undersurfaces. Note the small diameter fuselage roundel with narrow Yellow outer ring and the exceptionally broad fin stripes.

Spitfire Mk I, R6799, YT•D of 65 Sqn., Hornchurch, July 1940, flown by S/Ldr H C Sawyer.
Dark Earth and Dark Green uppersurfaces with duck egg green/Eau-de-Nil (?) undersurfaces. Note 'The East India Fund Flight' stencil below the starboard side canopy hood.

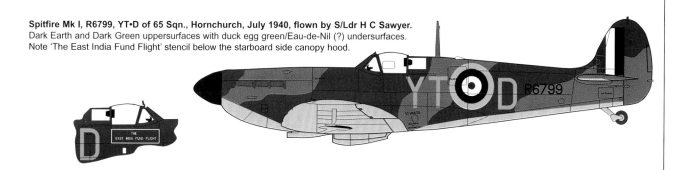

Spitfire Mk I, P9398, KL•B of 54 Sqn., Hornchurch, June 1940, flown by F/Lt A Deere.
Dark Earth and Dark Green uppersurfaces with duck egg green/Eau-de-Nil (?) undersurfaces. Note the 27 inch high fin stripes and the 'Kiwi' emblem under the port windscreen.

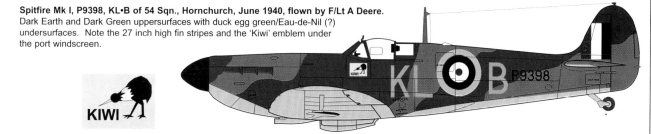

Note: All the shades on the undersurfaces are provisional and are based upon b&w photograph interpretation.

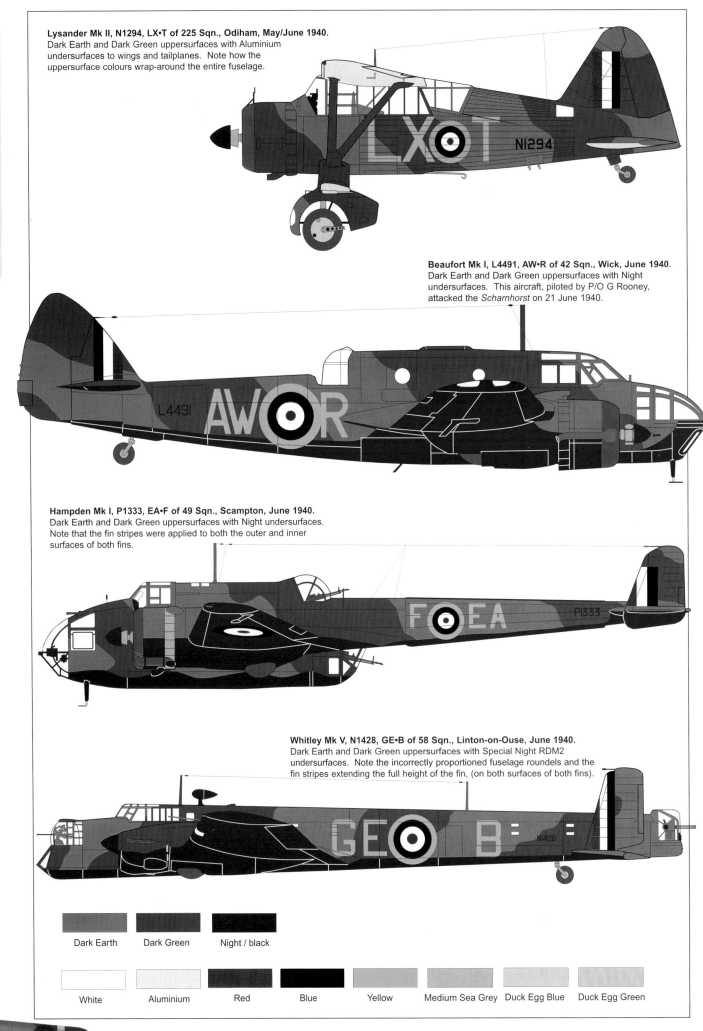

Lysander Mk II, N1294, LX•T of 225 Sqn., Odiham, May/June 1940.
Dark Earth and Dark Green uppersurfaces with Aluminium
undersurfaces to wings and tailplanes. Note how the
uppersurface colours wrap-around the entire fuselage.

Beaufort Mk I, L4491, AW•R of 42 Sqn., Wick, June 1940.
Dark Earth and Dark Green uppersurfaces with Night
undersurfaces. This aircraft, piloted by P/O G Rooney,
attacked the *Scharnhorst* on 21 June 1940.

Hampden Mk I, P1333, EA•F of 49 Sqn., Scampton, June 1940.
Dark Earth and Dark Green uppersurfaces with Night undersurfaces.
Note that the fin stripes were applied to both the outer and inner
surfaces of both fins.

Whitley Mk V, N1428, GE•B of 58 Sqn., Linton-on-Ouse, June 1940.
Dark Earth and Dark Green uppersurfaces with Special Night RDM2
undersurfaces. Note the incorrectly proportioned fuselage roundels and the
fin stripes extending the full height of the fin, (on both surfaces of both fins).

Dark Earth	Dark Green	Night / black

White	Aluminium	Red	Blue	Yellow	Medium Sea Grey	Duck Egg Blue	Duck Egg Green

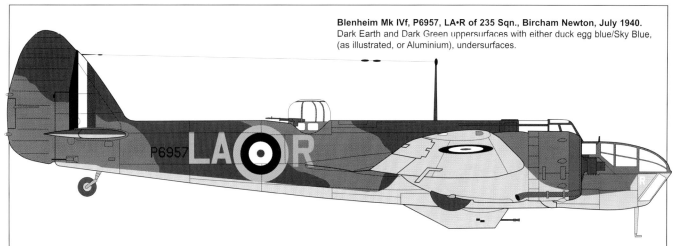

Blenheim Mk IVf, P6957, LA•R of 235 Sqn., Bircham Newton, July 1940.
Dark Earth and Dark Green uppersurfaces with either duck egg blue/Sky Blue,
(as illustrated, or Aluminium), undersurfaces.

Blenheim Mk IV, R3744, BL•K of 40 Sqn., Wyton, July 1940.
Dark Earth and Dark Green uppersurfaces with 'Sky' undersurfaces. This
aircraft, and the two Blenheims below, were built by Rootes, who may have had
quantities of a colour very similar to the correct shade of Sky, (albeit not to Type
S standard), which was a pale duck egg green shade and slightly glossy . Note
the individual aircraft letter in White.

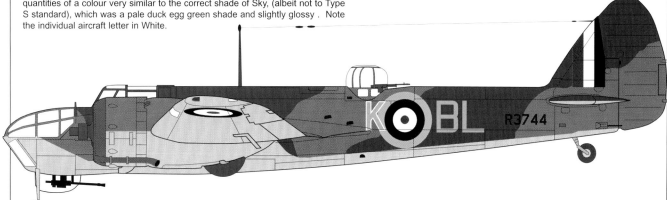

Blenheim Mk IV, R3821, UX•N of 82 (United Provinces) Sqn., Bodney, July 1941.
Dark Earth and Dark Green uppersurfaces with duck egg green/Sky undersurfaces.

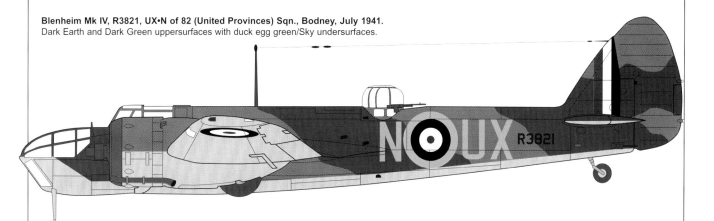

Blenheim Mk IV, R3741, VE•A of 110 Sqn., Wyton, July 1940.
Dark Earth and Dark Green uppersurfaces with duck egg
green/Sky undersurfaces. Note the individual aircraft
letter in White.

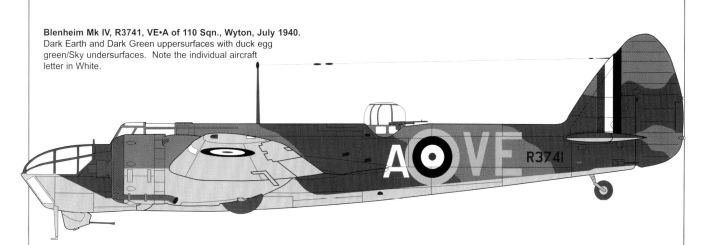

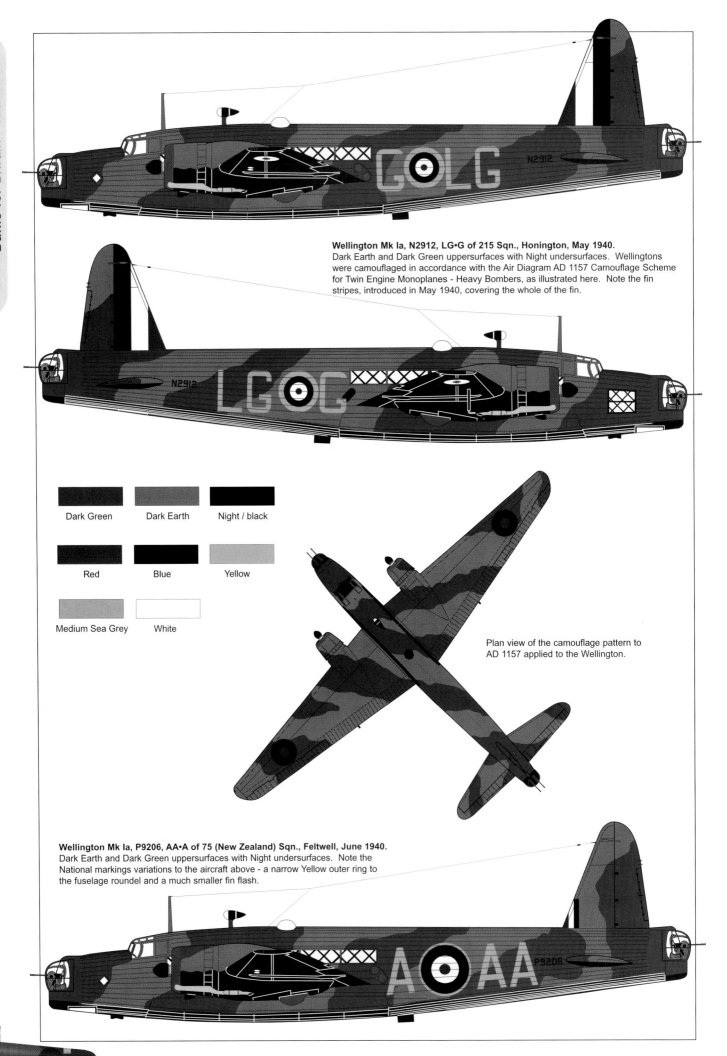

Wellington Mk Ia, N2912, LG•G of 215 Sqn., Honington, May 1940.
Dark Earth and Dark Green uppersurfaces with Night undersurfaces. Wellingtons were camouflaged in accordance with the Air Diagram AD 1157 Camouflage Scheme for Twin Engine Monoplanes - Heavy Bombers, as illustrated here. Note the fin stripes, introduced in May 1940, covering the whole of the fin.

Dark Green   Dark Earth   Night / black

Red   Blue   Yellow

Medium Sea Grey   White

Plan view of the camouflage pattern to AD 1157 applied to the Wellington.

Wellington Mk Ia, P9206, AA•A of 75 (New Zealand) Sqn., Feltwell, June 1940.
Dark Earth and Dark Green uppersurfaces with Night undersurfaces. Note the National markings variations to the aircraft above - a narrow Yellow outer ring to the fuselage roundel and a much smaller fin flash.

Long serving Hampden I, P1258, ZN•W of 106 Sqn., which served with this unit throughout 1940, and would have been progressively updated at Squadron level, which can be seen by the fact that the serial number has been painted around. Note how the fuselage roundel, thought to have been applied with Type S materials, stands out against the ultra-matt Special Night Finish. Aircrews would later complain how the fuselage roundel "lit up like a light bulb" when caught in the beam of a searchlight. This was because the Type S materials reflected more light than the surrounding Special Night camouflage.

masks could be used for the different colours and the resulting sharp boundaries would be accepted. The new Standard of Finish did not apply to the 'Special Night' black finish which was called for on the undersurfaces of the fuselage and wings of Night Bomber aircraft.

As it was not felt practicable to apply rigid inspection of the finish for either roughness or gloss at the aircraft manufacturing firms, roughness was to be estimated 'by feel' after a little skill had been gained by using the Lycopodium grain comparison method. This was done by sprinkling the surface locally with a few lycopodium spores, (lycopodium being a type of moss), and then examining it through a Coddington Lens which had a magnification of approximately 20x. Lycopodium spores have a diameter of approximately one thousandth of an inch and by comparison with these, the size of any protuberances on the surface could be estimated. By comparison, Gloss was not considered difficult to assess by eye.

If the finished surface was to be rubbed down, the following method was to be used. A strip of Hydro Durexsil No 400A abrasive paper, 3 inches wide by 11 inches long, was to be folded around a pad of sponge rubber approximately three quarters of an inch thick, 3 inches wide and 4 inches long. The pad was then to be held between the thumb and forefingers so that about 1 inch of the 3 inch width projected beyond the fingers

with the remainder of the pad lying in the palm of the hand.

The surface to be rubbed down was then to be wetted with water and the pad applied as if it were a paint brush using circular strokes with very light pressure. Care was to be taken not to touch rivet heads and to use the least possible pressure when passing over other projections. The surface should be kept wet, and a fresh area of the abrasive paper exposed at intervals as necessary.

After rubbing down, the surface was to be thoroughly cleaned with water and a scrubbing brush before being allowed to dry. Type S paints might have been introduced gradually from circa May/June/July 1940 onwards, and at roughly the same time, the requirement for the colour demarcation between camouflage colours to be a soft one was made no longer mandatory. As a consequence there is no clear picture as to which aircraft manufacturer followed which process, with which materials, and at what time.

Archaeological evidence does however show that Armstrong Whitworth were applying hard-edged camouflage using Dark Earth, Dark Green and Night using what appears to be the original standard matt paint in April 1940; whilst Glosters were applying Dark Earth and Dark Green camouflage to Hurricanes

with a sheen and a soft edge in July 1940. It is not easy however to tell whether the original matt paint was used then sanded down which would impart a slight sheen, or whether Type S materials were used. Until such time as more research into this matter can be carried out, the picture will remain unclear.

Where references to 'Type S' materials are made, these should not be confused with the appearance of the letter 'S' on any airframe stencilling which might appear below a DTD number. The use of the letter 'S' below a DTD number when applied to the airframe signifies the use of a Synthetic, as opposed to a Cellulose finish, which is signified by the use of the letter 'C'. Both Synthetic and Cellulose finishes could be made from the finely ground pigments which bestowed a Type S finish.

By the end of 1940, with the exception of Special Night, all aircraft camouflage paints whether Synthetic or Cellulose based were supposed to be manufactured using Type S materials.

All top coat camouflage and identification marking colours were manufactured to meet the same technical specifications. Clearly Hawkers, the manufacturer of this Hurricane of 615 Sqn, with P3811, KW•R in the background, pictured in late 1940, used the correct paints throughout for the camouflage scheme and the National markings.

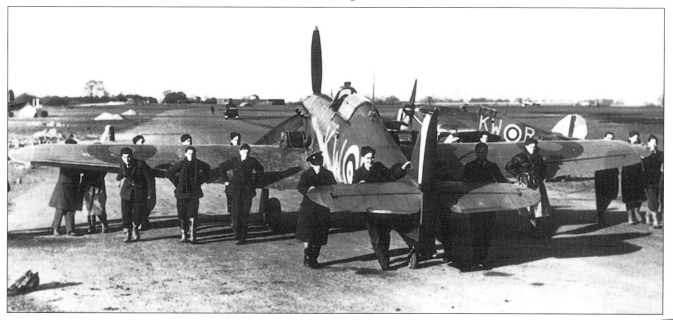

Anson Mk I, N9732, MK•V of 500 (County of Kent) Sqn., Detling, June 1940.
Dark Earth and Dark Green uppersurfaces with Aluminium undersurfaces. (see opposite for more details of N9732)

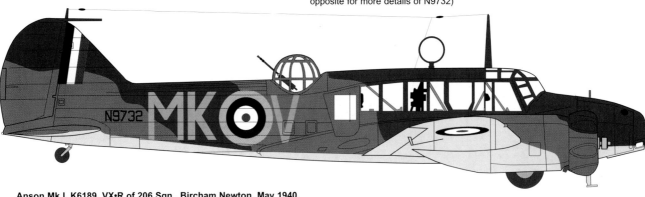

Anson Mk I, K6189, VX•R of 206 Sqn., Bircham Newton, May 1940.
Dark Earth and Dark Green uppersurfaces with Aluminium undersurfaces.
Note early sloping windscreen and underwing roundels placed at extreme wing tips.

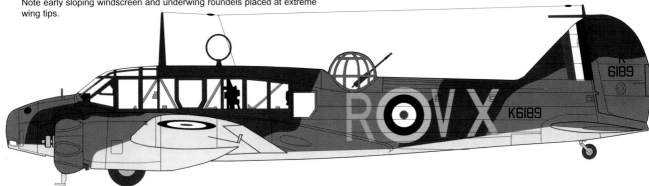

Anson Mk I, K6285, MW•F of 217 Sqn., St Eval, July 1940.
Dark Earth and Dark Green uppersurfaces with Aluminium undersurfaces.
Note, that whilst the Yellow outer ring to the fuselage roundel has been added, the fin stripes have yet to be applied.

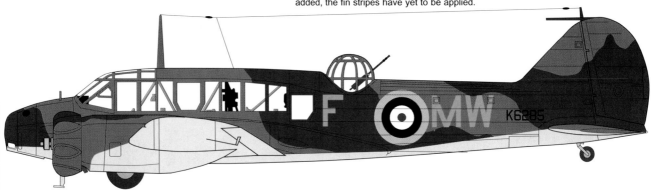

Anson Mk I, N9629, YG•E of 502 (Ulster) Sqn., Aldergrove, July 1940.
Dark Earth and Dark Green uppersurfaces, with Aluminium undersurfaces.
Note the small Red/White/Blue underwing roundels and the angle of the fin stripes following the rudder hinge line.

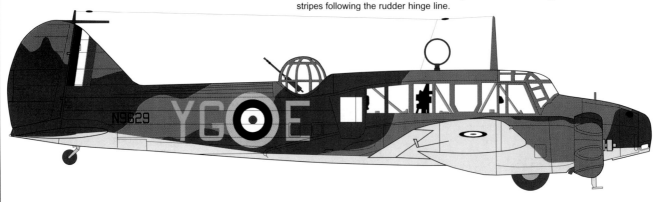

| Dark Earth | Dark Green | Aluminium | Red | Blue | Yellow | Medium Sea Grey | Dutch Navy silver grey |

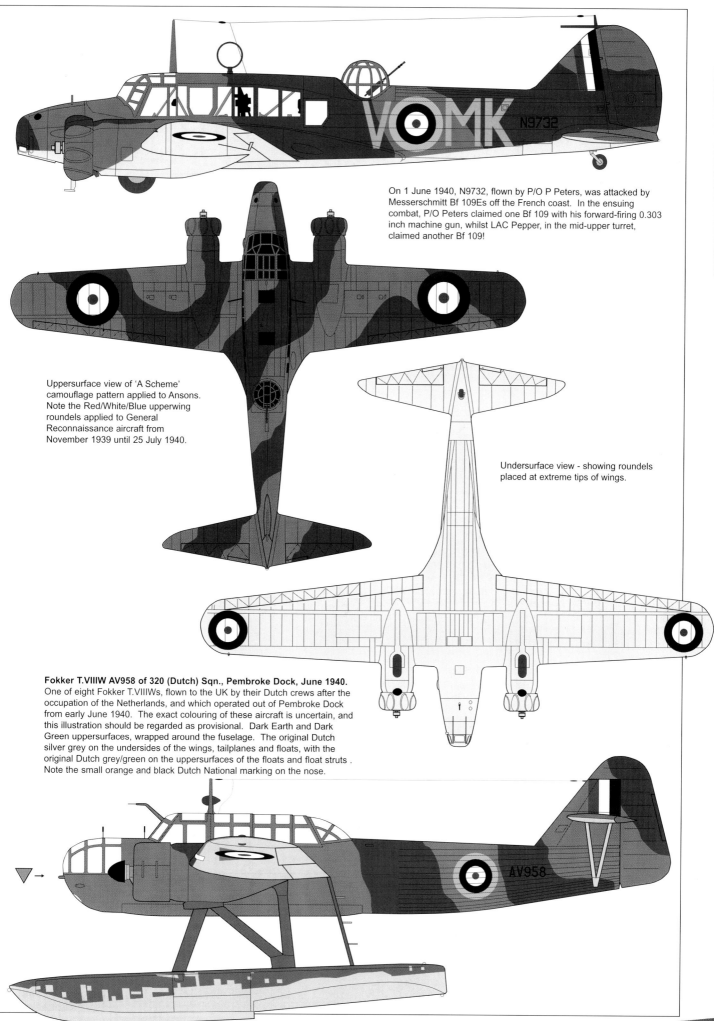

On 1 June 1940, N9732, flown by P/O P Peters, was attacked by Messerschmitt Bf 109Es off the French coast. In the ensuing combat, P/O Peters claimed one Bf 109 with his forward-firing 0.303 inch machine gun, whilst LAC Pepper, in the mid-upper turret, claimed another Bf 109!

Uppersurface view of 'A Scheme' camouflage pattern applied to Ansons. Note the Red/White/Blue upperwing roundels applied to General Reconnaissance aircraft from November 1939 until 25 July 1940.

Undersurface view - showing roundels placed at extreme tips of wings.

Fokker T.VIIIW AV958 of 320 (Dutch) Sqn., Pembroke Dock, June 1940.
One of eight Fokker T.VIIIWs, flown to the UK by their Dutch crews after the occupation of the Netherlands, and which operated out of Pembroke Dock from early June 1940. The exact colouring of these aircraft is uncertain, and this illustration should be regarded as provisional. Dark Earth and Dark Green uppersurfaces, wrapped around the fuselage. The original Dutch silver grey on the undersides of the wings, tailplanes and floats, with the original Dutch grey/green on the uppersurfaces of the floats and float struts. Note the small orange and black Dutch National marking on the nose.

PART 2

BATTLE FOR BRITAIN
May to December 1940

CHAPTER 5
DYNAMIC CHANGES May - June 1940

Despite the issue of AMO A.520/39, Coastal Command had continued to conduct trials to improve the recognition markings carried by British aircraft. During February 1940, an Anson aircraft of 16 Group was marked up with a yellow band around the roundel and a yellow band around the fin, and observation tests made. In its report to HQ. Coastal Command made by signal on 6 March 1940, 16 Group reported that the narrow band of yellow which had been applied around the roundel was remarkably conspicuous and greatly facilitated recognition. Because the yellow band around the roundel was visible some distance before the fin marking, the latter was considered superfluous.

The Air Ministry meanwhile were considering the implications of putting recognition markings on the tails of aircraft. At a meeting on 8 March, held at the Air Ministry, the question of recognition markings arose and C in C Fighter Command mentioned that he had heard from the Air Component in France that the markings applied to the rudders were proving a very effective identification feature. The Coastal Command representative then mentioned the work being done by 16 Group with regard to this matter.

After some discussion, the C in C Fighter Command agreed that the roundel showed up much more distinctly with the

Heading: One of a sequence of well-known photographs of 610 Sqn., purportedly taken in early June 1940, showing the yellow surrounds added to the original red/white/blue fuselage roundels, and the introduction of red/white/blue fin stripes. Note the rather 'dark' undersurface colour, thought to have been BS 381 (1930) Sky Blue.

Right: No 500 Sqn's Coastal Command Ansons, based at Detling, were very active during the Dunkirk evacuation, and were suitably marked with yellow outlined fuselage roundels and fin stripes as N5226, MK•E here shows.

yellow ring around the outside and that this ought to be a big help, but he appears to have thought that some kind of tail marking was also required.

On 3 April 1940, the Air Ministry wrote to Coastal Command to inform them that the idea of applying recognition markings to the tail of an aircraft was being considered, but that such markings could not be applied to the control surfaces because of the problems associated with mass balance.

The alternative suggested by the Air Ministry, was to carry markings on both sides of the fin and on the upper and lower surfaces of the fixed portion of the tailplane. Whilst a yellow fin was suggested, it was realised that this would defeat the object of camouflaging the aircraft in the first place. The Air Ministry requested that Coastal Command consider the idea of applying national markings on fixed surfaces, and reply with their views.

Evidently the idea of applying a yellow ring to the outside of the fuselage roundel and National markings to the fixed part of the fin found widespread approval within the Service, as on 1 May

1940, the Air Ministry sent signal X485 to all Commands, at Home and Overseas, amending the markings carried by RAF aircraft. Fuselage roundels were to be encircled with a yellow band the same width of the existing blue band. Vertical stripes of red, white and blue, each of the same width, were to be painted on the fins.

Because those aircraft in France had set a precedent of applying vertical stripes on the rudder, and this was perceived as causing problems with the rudder's balance, the signal stressed that the new stripe marking was to be applied to the fin. The only further detail given in the signal was that blue should be nearest the rudder, but clear of the hinge.

Because no detail on the size of the new marking was given, many different interpretations were made by the units themselves as they tried to comply with the new instructions. Roundels were modified with yellow bands of many different widths to suit the size of the aircraft they were being applied to, whilst the fin flash was also applied in many different variations, with some aircraft such as the Sunderland, having markings

which extended for the full height of the fin. This made for some very impressive markings!

Such was the confusion that on 11 May, a further signal, X740, was sent to amplify Signal X485. The new signal stated that the fin markings of three vertical stripes need not necessarily occupy the whole surface of the fin. It was sufficient that the width of the marking was to be such that it was to be clearly visible. On no account were the hinge points or moveable surfaces to be painted.

The instructions for modifying the fuselage roundels were also amplified. Aircraft with slim fuselages were to have the whole roundel reduced in size in order to accommodate the new yellow outer ring and prevent it encroaching on the upper or under surface of the fuselage. As a temporary measure, in order to obviate excessive work on operational aircraft, the existing roundels could be outlined with a narrow band of yellow where the space available made the application of a yellow band the same width as the blue band impractical.

Whilst this change was in the process of being made, on 10 May the German offensive in the West opened and the war entered a new phase. With British-based fighters now likely to find themselves

This Hurricane, P2923, VY.R was built by Glosters, and delivered to 15 MU on 28 May before being issued to 85 Sqn., on 11 June. Glosters continued to use the pre-war 'bright' identification colours in the National markings of its Hurricanes, such as P2923, until at least September. Note the thin Yellow outline that has been added to the original Red/White/Blue fin stripes which cover the entire fin area.

operating over France, on 15 May, the underwing markings of all home based fighter aircraft were revised by Signal X296. Roundels, consisting of a red centre, surrounded by rings of white and blue, all of equal width, were to be applied to the underside of both wings forthwith. The roundels were to be as large as possible but were to be kept clear of the ailerons.

Following the fighting which ultimately led to the beaches of Dunkirk, Signal X479 of 4 June made reference to Signal X296 of 15 May, before going on to state that the roundels on the underside of the port (Night painted) wing of all fighter aircraft were to be "encircled by a yellow band 'of convenient width' but not less than one quarter, or greater than the full width, of the blue band". It was permissible to 'break' the new yellow band in order to keep the aileron and its hinges

From 1 May 1940, the National markings of all British military aircraft were revised to include a yellow surround to the fuselage roundel and red/white/blue stripes on the tail fin, as illustrated on this Blenheim If, Day Fighter, L1105 of 219 Sqn. Note how the yellow outer ring has been painted 'around' the existing Medium Sea Grey code letters, and what appears to be a Night section under the starboard cowling from the previous Night undersurface bomber scheme, contrasting with the new duck egg green 'Sky' colour.

free from paint. This new marking was to be applied at the earliest possible moment.

Scarcely had this marking instruction had time to be assimilated by the fighter squadrons then they were assailed by a much more troublesome requirement, that of removing all undersurface identification markings and replacing them with a new camouflage colour, Duck Egg Blue (Sky Type S)!

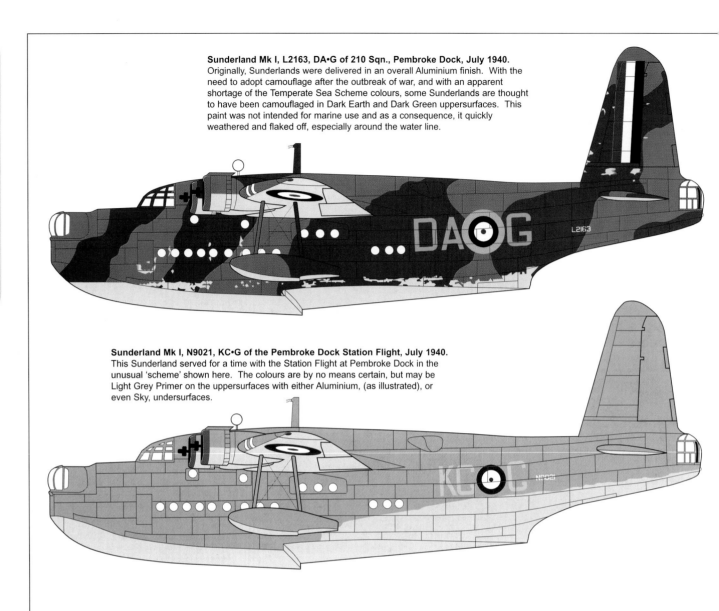

Sunderland Mk I, L2163, DA•G of 210 Sqn., Pembroke Dock, July 1940.
Originally, Sunderlands were delivered in an overall Aluminium finish. With the need to adopt camouflage after the outbreak of war, and with an apparent shortage of the Temperate Sea Scheme colours, some Sunderlands are thought to have been camouflaged in Dark Earth and Dark Green uppersurfaces. This paint was not intended for marine use and as a consequence, it quickly weathered and flaked off, especially around the water line.

Sunderland Mk I, N9021, KC•G of the Pembroke Dock Station Flight, July 1940.
This Sunderland served for a time with the Station Flight at Pembroke Dock in the unusual 'scheme' shown here. The colours are by no means certain, but may be Light Grey Primer on the uppersurfaces with either Aluminium, (as illustrated), or even Sky, undersurfaces.

Stranraer Mk I, K7295, BN•L of 240 Sqn., Pembroke Dock, October 1940.
Despite being a biplane, this aircraft would appear to have been finished in the Temperate Sea Scheme to AD 1164 for Twin Engine Monoplanes - General Reconnaissance (Flying Boats), of Extra Dark Sea Grey and Dark Slate Grey uppersurfaces, (without the shadow compensating Dark Sea Grey and Light Slate Grey areas). Undersurfaces were Night. Note the slightly incorrectly proportioned Red centre to the fuselage roundel.

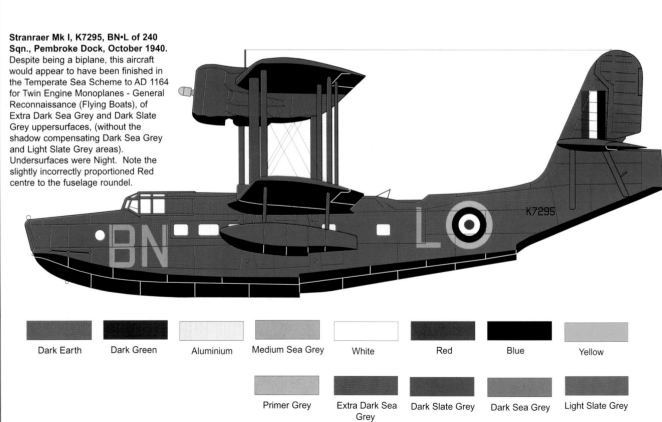

Dark Earth	Dark Green	Aluminium	Medium Sea Grey	White	Red	Blue	Yellow

Primer Grey	Extra Dark Sea Grey	Dark Slate Grey	Dark Sea Grey	Light Slate Grey

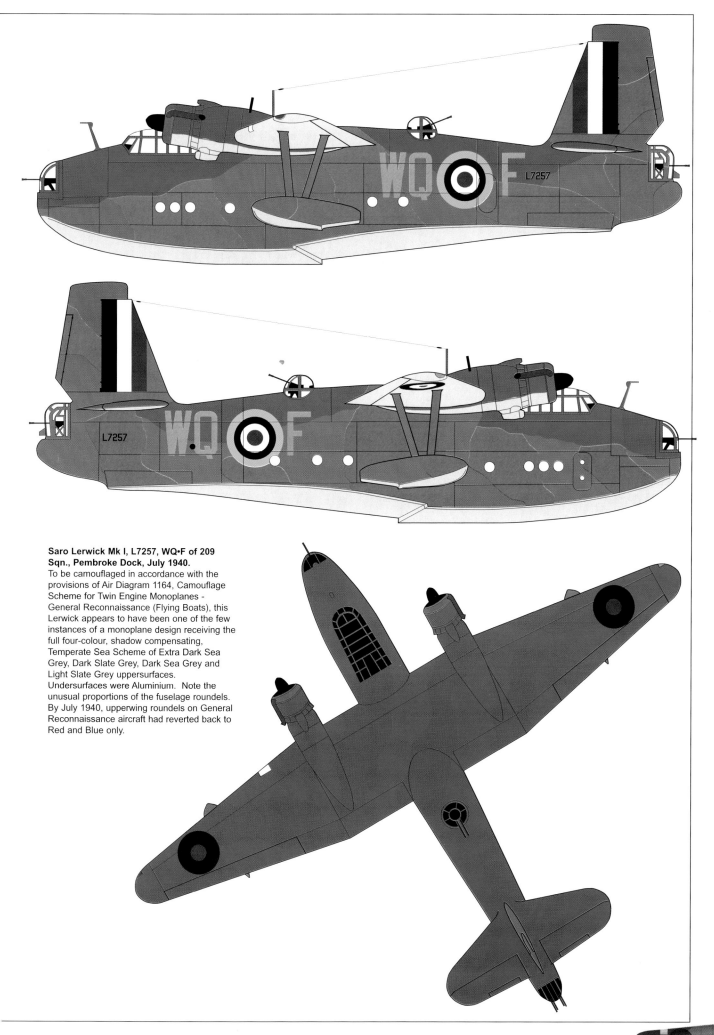

Saro Lerwick Mk I, L7257, WQ•F of 209 Sqn., Pembroke Dock, July 1940.
To be camouflaged in accordance with the provisions of Air Diagram 1164, Camouflage Scheme for Twin Engine Monoplanes - General Reconnaissance (Flying Boats), this Lerwick appears to have been one of the few instances of a monoplane design receiving the full four-colour, shadow compensating, Temperate Sea Scheme of Extra Dark Sea Grey, Dark Slate Grey, Dark Sea Grey and Light Slate Grey uppersurfaces. Undersurfaces were Aluminium. Note the unusual proportions of the fuselage roundels. By July 1940, upperwing roundels on General Reconnaissance aircraft had reverted back to Red and Blue only.

CHAPTER 6
DUCK EGG BLUE (SKY TYPE S)
May - December 1940

Following the introduction of Sky to the undersurfaces of Blenheims on the production line from about February 1940 onwards, the question of provisioning the new colour in adequate quantities appears to have begun making itself felt.

It has already been shown that paint which met the new Type S material specification was unavailable and that as a consequence the specification of DTD 63A was revised to make it less glossy so that it became known as 'DTD 63A with reduced gloss'.

If the supply situation was difficult with 'Sky to DTD 63A with reduced gloss' being applied to just one aircraft type, the situation became infinitely worse from early June when the use of Sky on Fighter Command aircraft was authorised.

The introduction of Sky to the under surfaces of fighter aircraft can be said to have begun from 6 June 1940. On this date the Air Ministry sent Signal X915 which stated that all undersurfaces of fighter aircraft, (that is the mainplanes, fuselage, and tailplanes), were to be doped to Sky Type S. All roundels on the undersides of mainplanes were to be removed. All previous instructions regarding painting and marking on under surfaces of fighter aircraft were cancelled.

This immediately caused problems as the fighter squadrons had absolutely no idea what colour Sky Type S was. The Air

Ministry tried to get around this problem by sending a signal to all concerned on 7 June, which said that, "the colour of camouflage Sky Type S, repeat S, may be described as Duck Egg Blueish Green".

This is the earliest use of any variation of the term 'Duck Egg Blue (Sky Type S)' found by the author, and it would seem that whoever wrote the original signal did not really know whether the colour he was describing was a 'blue' or a 'green'!

The Air Ministry could order what it liked, but it would appear that even supplies of Sky to DTD 63A with reduced gloss, appear to have been almost impossible to obtain, as, on 10 June, Signal X348 cancelled X915 of 6 June pending further instructions. This signal was followed by Signal X349 a short time later that same day, which stated that due to only limited supplies of Sky Type S dope to DTD 63, being available, fighters were to continue to operate with the black and white colour scheme until supplies of Sky Type S became available. Here clearly, the element of confusion was beginning to take hold, with the two different material specifications being perceived as one and the same thing, quite apart from the confusing colour

terminology which was already abroad!

Whilst the fighter squadrons were contemplating the latest changes in their camouflage and markings, the aircraft manufacturers were also being informed of the changes. On 11 June, Glosters were informed that they were to proceed with the painting on the undersurfaces of all fighter aircraft with Sky Type S instead of the present black and white colour scheme. The undersurfaces were to be read as meaning wings, fuselage and tail. The Sky colour was to extend up the sides of the fuselage as indicated on Air Diagrams 1160 and 1176 which were applicable to single and twin engined aircraft respectively. Neither roundels nor identification serial numbers were required at that time, and the change in colouring was to come into effect on all production aircraft at the earliest possible moment subject to there being no delay in delivery.

On 6 June, the same day as the first signal ordering the introduction of Sky on the undersurfaces of Day Fighters was sent out, the MAP wrote to the RAE with regard to the ruling allowing its introduction which had just been given by the Deputy Chief of the Air Staff which ruled that all fighter aircraft in the future

Heading: When compared with its fellow 25 Sqn Blenheim Mk If fighters in the background, this early delivery Beaufighter, R2069, as yet without an individual aircraft letter, has a comparatively dark undersurface which may be suggestive of a duck egg blue shade. The degree of shine visible on the undercarriage door of the Beaufighter perhaps suggests the use of DTD 63A with reduced gloss.

Right: In contrast to the Beaufighter in the heading photograph, these Defiants of 264 Sqn have what appears to be a much lighter undersurface colour which has been reported to be a "rich duck egg green".

Blenheims continued to leave the production line in what was 'supposed' to be Sky, but archaeological evidence shows that at least on *some* occasions, what might be termed a 'rich duck egg green' was applied, as may well be the case here on R3612, BL·V of 40 Sqn. Note the underwing roundels - dating the photograph to post 11 August 1940 - and the individual aircraft letter outlined in white, a characteristic of both this unit and 15 Sqn who also flew Blenheims.

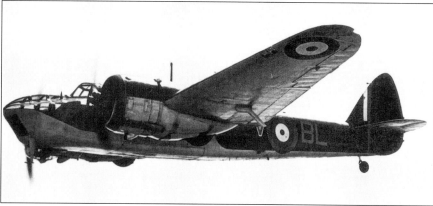

were to have Sky Type S paint on their undersurfaces instead of the then current black and white scheme.

No problem was anticipated with new production aircraft, but as the new finish would also be applied to aircraft already in service, it was thought that there might be trouble on two scores. Firstly that the Sky paint would not spray well over black; and secondly, once again worries about the weight of paint being applied to ailerons upsetting their balance re-appeared. Bearing these points in mind, the RAE was asked for advice as to whether the repainting could be done in service, and if so, what materials would be necessary.

Answers to these questions could not have been long in being supplied, as on 14 June, the Air Ministry informed everyone concerned that aircraft which were received from the contractors with black and white paint schemes could be sprayed over with not more than two coats of Sky Type S. Where this was done, to avoid mass balance problems with the ailerons, the existing paint was to be removed before re-spraying. This was to be done with Dope Solvent, Stores ref 33B/141. Service units were warned not to try to apply materials to DTD 308 on top of materials to DTD 314, or to try mixing these materials in any attempt that might be made to mix a Sky colour locally.

Whilst the fighter squadrons of Fighter Command were clear on their instructions with regard to repainting their aircraft's undersurfaces, the fighter squadrons in Coastal Command were not. Following the original Air Ministry Signal X915 of 6 June, the long range Blenheim fighter squadrons in Coastal Command had thought that the new undersurface colouring and marking instructions applied to them as well. HQ Coastal Command however had a different view. On 7 June, Signal ASD/373 was sent to all concerned notifying them that all Blenheim aircraft in Coastal Command would conform to the standard General Reconnaissance markings. This necessitated fighter Blenheims having their black and white markings removed and replaced by an Aluminium finish.

As on every Fighter Command squadron, such a change necessitated a

Lysanders were originally delivered with their Dark Earth/Dark Green camouflage wrapped right the way around the fuselage, and the undersurfaces of the wings and tailplanes finished in Aluminium. This Mk II, L4798, HB·X of 239 Sqn., has clearly been repainted, but in what colour it is impossible to tell.

great deal of work by the ground crews, Coastal Command seem to have negated this slightly by having a travelling band of aircraft finishers who travelled from station to station carrying out the required changes as they went. On 18 June, HQ 43 Group wrote a letter to HQ Coastal Command, to inform them that at Bircham Newton, 43 Group had approximately eighteen Blenheim fighters which were required to be camouflaged silver on their undersurfaces. It was requested that the services of a similar party to one which had visited West Raynham be made available to re-spray them.

Whilst Coastal Command sorted *their* problems out, problems remained for Fighter Command and the aircraft industry in trying to obtain supplies of Sky. Over a month after its supposed introduction, on 8 July, the Ministry of Aircraft Production sent a circular to all the Resident Technical Officers in the aircraft factories with regard to the under surface colour of Day Fighters. This was to the effect that the Director of Operational Requirements had ruled in a minute dated 11 June 1940, that the colours used on the undersurfaces of Day Fighters were no longer to be of the normal type, but in future were to be of a new smooth quality. Incorporation of this new requirement was entirely dependent upon stocks of Type S materials becoming available, but when they did become available, the materials were to be introduced to the production line as soon as possible and the works drawings

were to be amended accordingly. The new colour would be Sky Type S and be available to specifications DTD 83A, DTD 308, and DTD 314.

Following the withdrawal of the British forces from the Continent, some concern was expressed within the Air Ministry as to the large number of aircraft which had been left behind. The expressed concern was about the possibility of some of these aircraft being flown by German crews on operations over Britain. As a result of these concerns, a Postagram dated 20 July was sent from the Air Ministry to all home and overseas Commands, Admiralty, RNAS, War Office, Anti-Aircraft Command and the MAP, which advised the recipients that reports had been received that the Germans might be operating British types of aircraft. All concerned were to be notified of the enclosed detailed description of the authorised colours and markings on British aircraft. This same Postagram was apparently circulated to the aircraft manufacturers as DTD Technical Circular No 75 on 25 July.

In the section which dealt with the undersurfaces, fighters were to be "Painted duck egg blueish green (Sky Type S); and bombers and torpedo bombers were to be painted black with the exception of Blenheim bombers which were to be painted Duck-egg blueish green".

Even while the Postagram was being prepared for distribution by the DTD, a conference was held at the Air Ministry on 23 July 1940 to consider aircraft

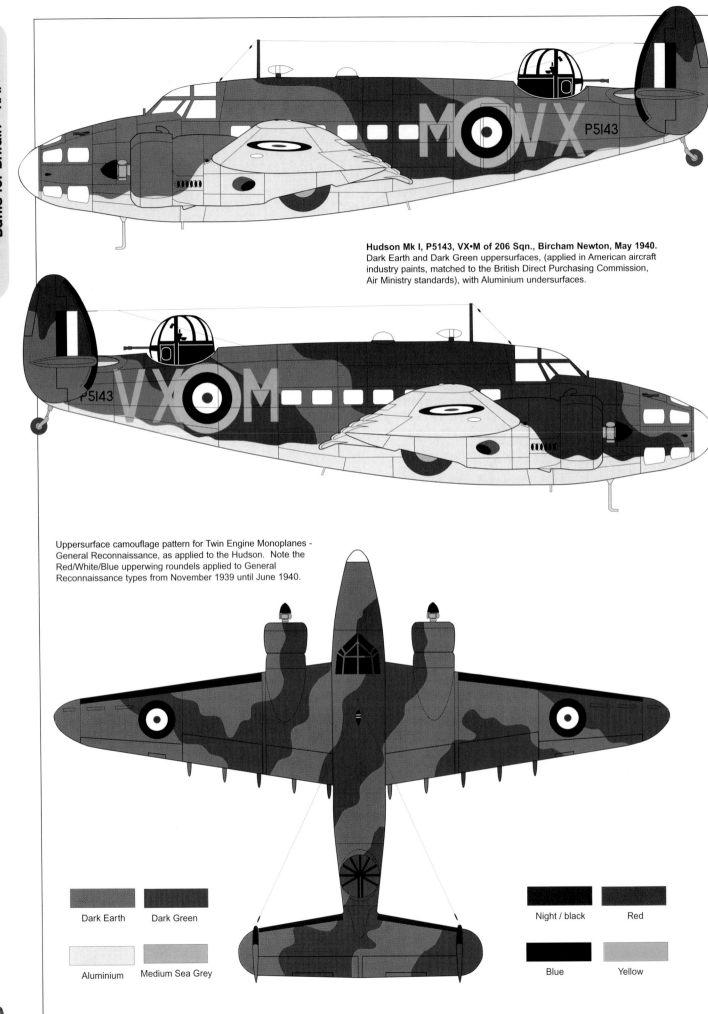

Hudson Mk I, P5143, VX•M of 206 Sqn., Bircham Newton, May 1940.
Dark Earth and Dark Green uppersurfaces, (applied in American aircraft industry paints, matched to the British Direct Purchasing Commission, Air Ministry standards), with Aluminium undersurfaces.

Uppersurface camouflage pattern for Twin Engine Monoplanes - General Reconnaissance, as applied to the Hudson. Note the Red/White/Blue upperwing roundels applied to General Reconnaissance types from November 1939 until June 1940.

Dark Earth   Dark Green

Aluminium   Medium Sea Grey

Night / black   Red

Blue   Yellow

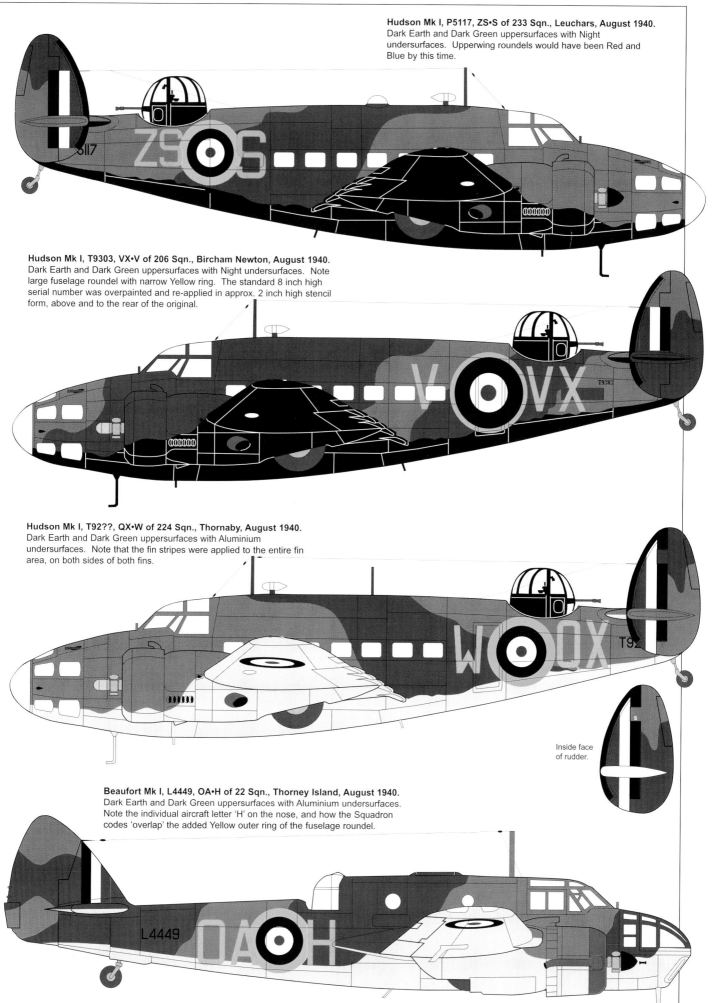

Hudson Mk I, P5117, ZS•S of 233 Sqn., Leuchars, August 1940.
Dark Earth and Dark Green uppersurfaces with Night undersurfaces. Upperwing roundels would have been Red and Blue by this time.

Hudson Mk I, T9303, VX•V of 206 Sqn., Bircham Newton, August 1940.
Dark Earth and Dark Green uppersurfaces with Night undersurfaces. Note large fuselage roundel with narrow Yellow ring. The standard 8 inch high serial number was overpainted and re-applied in approx. 2 inch high stencil form, above and to the rear of the original.

Hudson Mk I, T92??, QX•W of 224 Sqn., Thornaby, August 1940.
Dark Earth and Dark Green uppersurfaces with Aluminium undersurfaces. Note that the fin stripes were applied to the entire fin area, on both sides of both fins.

Inside face
of rudder.

Beaufort Mk I, L4449, OA•H of 22 Sqn., Thorney Island, August 1940.
Dark Earth and Dark Green uppersurfaces with Aluminium undersurfaces. Note the individual aircraft letter 'H' on the nose, and how the Squadron codes 'overlap' the added Yellow outer ring of the fuselage roundel.

colourings and markings with a view to achieving the maximum degree of standardisation.

At this meeting it was pointed out that at that time, the RAF was using two different colours, (described as duck-egg blue and silver), which were used to achieve the same effect. It was agreed that duck-egg blue was a better colour scheme for undersurfaces than silver, and that there was no reason why aircraft with silver undersurfaces should not conform to the duck egg blue colour scheme. It was agreed that all types of aircraft whose undersurfaces were silver should change over to Sky Type S as soon as supplies of this material became available

That said however, it was also agreed that the colour on the undersurfaces of operational types of aircraft should not be rigidly laid down, but that it should be left to the discretion of the Operational Commands to paint the undersurfaces of their aircraft either duck-egg blue (Sky Type S) or matt black, according to the operational role of the aircraft.

The decisions made at the conference were circulated to all Commands at home and abroad, 22 and 61 Groups, the Royal Naval Air Service, the Admiralty, the War Office and Anti-Aircraft Command as well as a large number of departments within the Air Ministry, by a letter dated 11 August accompanied by an appendix.

Paragraph 3 of the appendix dealt with aircraft undersurfaces. The colouring of the undersurfaces were to be as follows.-
(i) Operational aircraft. The under surfaces of all operational aircraft were to be either matt black or duck egg blue and could be either one or the other at the discretion of individual Commands to meet operational requirements. The following classes of aircraft were to be produced with duck egg blue under surfaces:- Fighters, Army co-operation, General Reconnaissance, Torpedo bombers, Blenheim bombers, Close support bombers, Troop carriers, and bomber transports.

This appendix was also circulated to the aircraft manufacturers as a DTD

Technical Circular, No 83, on 23 August. In the accompanying letter, the recipients were asked to note that in paragraph 3(i) "....provision is made for either matt black or duck egg blue, ie Sky Type S....", so there can be no doubt that the colour which was supposed to be applied was Sky.

It can be deduced from the repeated references to Sky Type S being used, when supplies become available, which appear in documents throughout June and July of 1940, that supplies of Sky to either DTD 63A with reduced gloss, or DTD 83A, DTD 308, and DTD 314 Type S, were generally not available to fighter squadrons during those months.

Eyewitness accounts of the period June/August 1940, suggest that there were various shades of green, blue, and grey being used on Day Fighter under surfaces before Sky became the most commonly seen colour from late-August onwards.

Archaeological evidence suggests that what would appear to have happened is that, following Signal X915 of 6 June 1940, the fighter squadrons began to indent the stores organisation for supplies of Sky Type S. However, as supplies of this colour and material were difficult, if not impossible, to obtain, they were forced to use something else instead.

Documentary evidence shows that DTD 63A with reduced gloss, was the material specification used on the Blenheim, and that this same material was intended for use on fighters, but what of the colour? It might be reasonable to assume that when confronted with demands for a colour and or material which *was not* available, the paint manufacturers would supply whatever *was* available instead.

Colours to material specification DTD 63 were available before the war, the standard itself being revised to DTD 63A in April 1939. Unfortunately the specification does not go into any detail about what colours were available, but a contemporary companion specification, DTD 260A which was reprinted in August 1940 does. Paragraph 3 'Colour' states that the standard was to be one of the British Standard colours listed in the

latest issue of British Standard Specification 381.

To a large extent, specifications DTD 63A and DTD 260A were complementary, DTD 63A being a material specification for Cellulose Enamels and Primer for use on metals and timber, whilst DTD 260A was a material specification for Pigmented Oil Varnishes, and Primer also, for use on metals and timber. Therefore it might be reasonable to assume that the colours listed in the latest issue of British Standard Specification 381 were also available in materials to DTD 63A as well. Indeed, when DTD 63A was superseded by DTD 63B in June 1947, the new standard did state that the colours available to the specification were those of BSS 381 in its latest issue. Whilst not conclusive in itself, this revision might be an official acknowledgement of what had been a long standing practice within the aircraft finish industry.

British Standard Specification 381, 'Schedule of Colours for Ready Mixed Paints' was issued in November 1930 and was still current in 1940. Examination of the 1930 edition of BSS 381 appears to offer two colours which might possibly have been used, which would account for the subjective colloquial descriptions of the under surface colour(s) reported by eyewitnesses at the time of 'duck egg blue', and 'a rich duck egg green'. These colours were BSS 381 (1930) No 1 Sky Blue, a light blue-green colour which could be described as a duck egg blue; and No 16 Eau-de-Nil which could be considered to be a duck egg green.

That these two colours were used in place of Sky appears to be confirmed by the available archaeological evidence. Visits were made to a number of aviation museums throughout Kent and Sussex, during which recovered wreckage of aircraft lost during 1940 was examined, and an attempt was made to match any paint which remained in situ.

This matching is shown in progress in photographs 6 and 7 inside front cover.

Matching the samples of paint still adhering to the wreckage of several aircraft revealed that the 'rich duck egg green' had several minor variations in colour whilst all were consistently smooth and slightly glossy, whilst only one shade of blue which was also smooth and slightly glossy, appears to have been used. Comparison with various colour standards revealed that all the minor variations in the 'rich duck egg green' were near, if not exact, matches for BSS 381 (1930) No 16 Eau-de-Nil; whilst the 'duck egg blue' was a match for BSS 381 (1930) No1 Sky Blue.

When the dates the individual aircraft

In-service repaints could sometimes take an unusual turn. This Hurricane, P2754, YB·W of 17 Sqn., is typical of this Squadron's aircraft during June-August, in that when the undersurfaces were repainted, the new colour was often extended up the lower cowling sides, along the leading edges of the wings, and even on to the spinner.

Right: No 222 Sqn may have been one of the units to variously paint the undersurfaces of its Spitfires in both 'duck egg blue' (BSS 381 No 1 Sky Blue) and 'duck egg green' (BSS No 16 Eau-de-Nil), but what P9323, ZD·F may have been finished in may have to remain open to question!

Below: Whilst Spitfire Mk I, R6597, UM·V of 152 Sqn., photographed in November in typical late-1940 scheme and markings, shows a much lighter undersurface colour that was possibly BSS No 16 Eau-de-Nil. Note the underwing roundels were applied at either MU or Squadron level.

were lost was set down in chronological order alongside the colour paint which was on them at the time, a pattern suggested itself.

As can be seen, Sky only becomes common from mid-September onwards. Whilst there are two examples of Sky being used from mid-August, substitute colours are by far the most common up to mid-September. Whilst such a small sample cannot be regarded as conclusive, it does appear to reflect the picture obtained from the documents consulted and eyewitness accounts. It is unfortunate that more aircraft from June and July have not been recovered as this would no doubt help give an even better picture of events.

The paints used instead of Sky therefore seem to be of three colours. The first is Sky Grey. This was surprisingly common given that little if

any mention of it being used on RAF aircraft at this time has been made in previously published literature. Given that this is the case, it is perhaps time to re-assess eyewitness accounts of fighters being coloured half black and half 'light grey' prior to the introduction of Sky.

Besides the aircraft known to have carried Sky Grey listed below, it was also found on the remains of two separate but unidentifiable aircrafts' remains. Photograph 12 on the inside back cover, clearly shows the original Aluminium finish where the Sky Grey has flaked off. It may or may not be of significance that both the unidentified remains on which this colour was found were starboard elevators. Unfortunately it is impossible to definitely link these two elevators to

aircraft lost during 1940, but it is believed that they were.

The second colour has been described in the table below as 'Eau-de-Nil'. Examination of wreckage listed shows that there were several slightly different shades of the Eau-de-Nil colour. These range from an exact match for BSS 381 (1930) No 16 Eau-de-Nil, to FS 595B 14533 and 14449. Lest the reader without access to either an edition of BSS 381 or FS 595 think these are widely differing colours, it must be stated that they are not. The difference between BSS 381 (1930) No 16 Eau-de-Nil, FS 595B 14533 and FS 595B 14449 is so slight, that samples of each colour have to be put right up against one another in order to perceive the difference. This slight difference is possibly indicative of supplies of paint being obtained from different manufacturers, or being from different batches of paint from the same manufacturer. In all cases, the surface finish was smooth and quite glossy, being indicative of materials supplied to DTD 63A with reduced gloss.

One specific example where an 'Eau-de-Nil' colour has been used where Sky was called for, was Spitfire P9469 of 222 Sqn coded ZD•T which was lost on 7 October 1940; the remains of which are held by the Robertsbridge Aviation Society. According to the Aircraft Movement Card, Air Ministry Form 78, this aircraft was completed and first flew on 12 April 1940. It was then delivered to 24 MU on 15 April. From there it was put on the strength of 602 Sqn on 20 May. At this time it would probably have been finished in the Night and White scheme which was superseded on 6 June. The aircraft remained on the strength of 602 Sqn for just one day, being transferred to 222 Sqn on 21 May where it remained until it was lost in combat on 7 October.

Whilst no trace of the Night and White scheme was to be seen on the pieces of the aircraft examined, the metal panel shown in the colour photographs, 7 and 8, on the inside front cover, was found to have three layers of paint on it!

The first layer of paint which was next to the metal appeared on the surface to be an unidentified brown colour. However, when one of the Society members carefully removed a loose flake of this paint, the side which had been next to

Aircraft	Date of loss	Undersurface Colour
Hurricane, P3479, 56 Sqn	13 August	Sky
Hurricane, V6581, 85 Sqn	31 August	BSS 381 (1930) No 1 Sky Blue
Hurricane, P2946, 253 Sqn	2 September	Sky
Hurricane, P3310, 73 Sqn	5 September	'Eau-de-Nil'
Hurricane, R4230, 249 Sqn	7 September	'Eau-de-Nil'
Spitfire, P9467, 603 Sqn	7 September	Sky Grey
Hurricane, P2728, 607 Sqn	7 September	'Blue Grey'
Spitfire, X4325, 41 Sqn	11 September	Sky Grey
Spitfire, R6625	14 September	Sky
Hurricane, V7357	17 September	Sky
Spitfire, X4410	20 September	Sky
Spitfire, X4422, 92 Sqn	27 September	Sky
Spitfire, P9469, 222 Sqn	7 October	'Eau-de-Nil and BSS 381 (1930) No.1 Sky Blue'
Hurricane, V6722, 501 Sqn	8 October	Sky
Hurricane, L1928, 253 Sqn	10 October	Sky
Spitfire, P7303, 616 Sqn	27 October	Sky
Hurricane, V6879, 605 Sqn	1 November	Sky
Blenheim, T2161, 82 Sqn	4 December	'Eau-de-Nil'

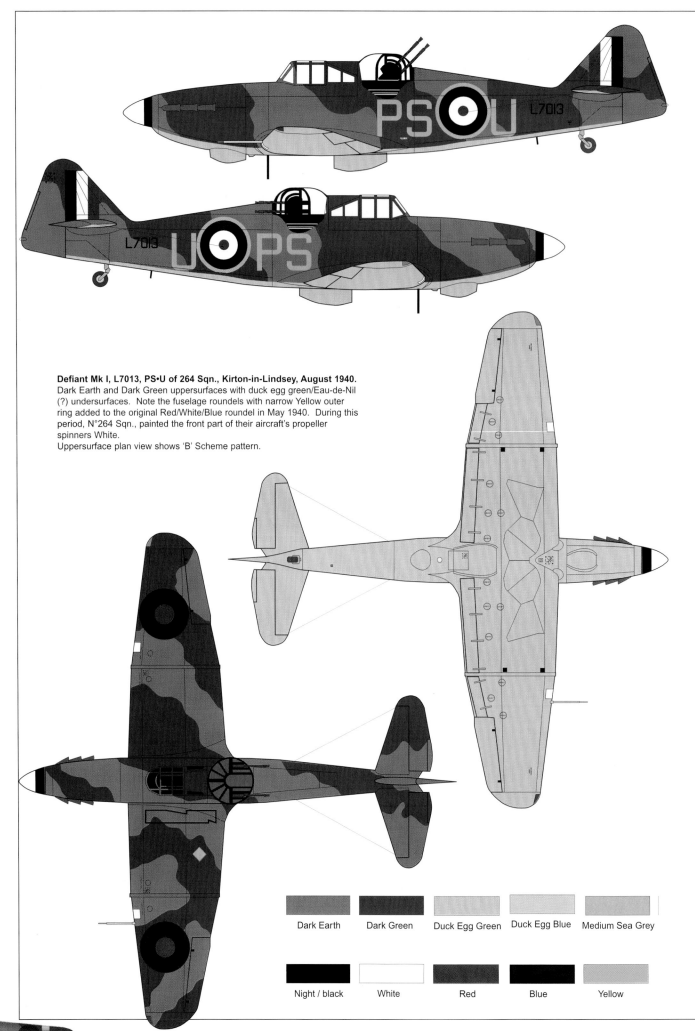

Defiant Mk I, L7013, PS•U of 264 Sqn., Kirton-in-Lindsey, August 1940.
Dark Earth and Dark Green uppersurfaces with duck egg green/Eau-de-Nil
(?) undersurfaces. Note the fuselage roundels with narrow Yellow outer
ring added to the original Red/White/Blue roundel in May 1940. During this
period, N°264 Sqn., painted the front part of their aircraft's propeller
spinners White.
Uppersurface plan view shows 'B' Scheme pattern.

Dark Earth	Dark Green	Duck Egg Green	Duck Egg Blue	Medium Sea Grey
Night / black	White	Red	Blue	Yellow

Defiant Mk I, N1535, PS•A of 264 Sqn., Hornchurch, August 1940.
Dark Earth and Dark Green uppersurfaces with duck egg green/Eau-de-Nil (?) undersurfaces. Flown by S/Ldr P Hunter, (note the Squadron Leader's pennant beneath the cockpit), and Sgt F King. This aircraft was shot down on 24 August 1940.

Defiant Mk I, N1636, PS•R of 264 Sqn., Hornchurch, August 1940.
Dark Earth and Dark Green uppersurfaces with duck egg green/Eau-de-Nil (?) undersurfaces. Note that on all Defiant aircraft, the framework to the Boulton Paul four-gun turret was painted Night.

Defiant Mk I, L7026, PS•V of 264 Sqn., Hornchurch, August 1940.
Dark Earth and Dark Green uppersurfaces with duck egg green/Eau-de-Nil (?) undersurfaces. Flown by P/O P L Kenner and P/O C E Johnson. This aircraft was shot down on 28 August 1940.

DEfiant Mk I, L7036, TW•H of 141 Sqn., Grangemouth, June 1940.
Dark Earth and Dark Green uppersurfaces with duck egg blue/Sky Blue (?) undersurfaces. Note the narrow Yellow outer ring to the fuselage roundel.

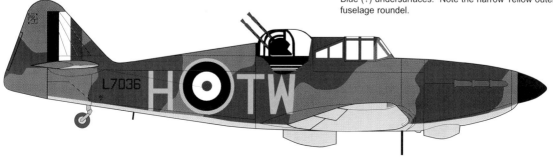

Note all undersurface colours should be regarded as provisional.

the metal was found to be an exact match for BSS 381 (1930) No 16 Eau-de-Nil.

The second layer of paint was the green colour, shown being matched to FS 14449 in photograph 7 on the inside front cover. This had a very smooth finish which whilst not a full gloss, did hold some degree of shine. This might be indicative of the use of DTD 63A 'with reduced gloss'.

The top coat of paint matched BSS 381 (1930) No 1 Sky Blue - traces of this colour also being found on the tail wheel shown in photographs 5 and 6 on the inside front cover. This, it will be recalled, is a pale blue with just a hint of green which could colloquially be described as 'duck egg blue'. This was also found to be smooth and shiny, and possibly indicative of the use of DTD 63A 'with reduced gloss'.

Thus it would appear that P9469 was repainted in service hands at least three times during the summer of 1940 without ever actually carrying the correct colour!

If the Service could not get supplies of Sky Type S, it would seem that the aircraft manufacturers were little better off. Whilst eyewitness accounts suggest that Blenheims built by Bristols in the early part of 1940 were finished in Sky, albeit to DTD 63 with reduced gloss, archaeological evidence shows that the colour which was applied to Blenheim undersurfaces on the production line by Rootes was not.

The evidence for this is provided by the remains of Blenheim Mk IV, T2161 of 82 Sqn held by Brenzett Aviation Museum. This particular aircraft was built by Rootes and first delivered to the RAF on 10 August 1940, at a time when according to the currently accepted view, Sky was well established both on the production line and in service. The paint which remains on the wreckage however, is quite unlike the correct shade of Sky, being an excellent match for FS 595B 14533. This is a near match for BSS 381 (1930) No 16 Eau-de-Nil. The surface finish appears to be very smooth and quite glossy, apparently once again indicating the use of materials to DTD

63A with reduced gloss.

Anyone using a current edition of BSS 381C to look up these colours should note that while No 216 Eau-de-Nil remains unaltered from No 16 in the 1930 edition of BSS 381, the current No 101 Sky Blue is just a little bit darker than No 1 Sky Blue in the 1930 edition. (The numbering system was altered in the 1948 edition.)

Of course it is also possible that individual units mixed their own paints, but at the time of writing, no official documentation on this subject had been found by the author. As it has already been mentioned that the Service was advised not to try mixing materials to DTD 308 with those of DTD 314 to this end, it is likely that this did take place although to what result remains unknown.

It would therefore seem that Air Ministry demands for Sky Type S were met by the paint manufacturing firms by the closest colours and materials which were available at that time in any quantity, namely BSS 381 (1930) No 1 Sky Blue and No 16 Eau-de-Nil to DTD 63A with reduced gloss, whilst several aircraft used Sky Grey. Sky Type S appears to have started to become available about the middle of August, and from mid-September onwards it appears to have become well established in service.

After the upheavals of the summer and autumn, AMO A.926 - Aircraft Colouring and Recognition Markings, was issued on 12 December 1940. In this AMO the under surfaces of operational aircraft were to be either matt black or duck egg blue at the discretion of Commands to meet operational requirements. The following classes of aircraft were to be produced with duck egg blue (Sky Type S) under surfaces:- Day Fighters, Blenheim bombers, Army Co-operation types, Close support bombers, General Reconnaissance aircraft, Troop carriers, Torpedo bombers, and Bomber transports. Day Fighters were to be coloured 'black' on the under surface of the port wing by aircraft storage units before delivery to Fighter Command units.

The issue of this AMO caused some

consternation at the RAE. On 21 December a letter was sent to the Air Ministry in which the RAE took issue with several of the points covered in the AMO. Amongst these points were the terms used to describe the undersurface colours, ie 'duck egg blue (Sky Type S)' and 'matt black'.

The RAE was of the opinion that the term 'duck egg blue' should not be used as in the RAE pattern book the colour used for this purpose was called 'Sky', the term 'Sky Type S' should just be 'Sky' as all colours were now of Type S; and the use of the term 'matt black' did not make it clear whether 'Night' or 'Special Night' were being referred to as both were matt colours. It is perhaps significant that when AMO A.926 was amended in January 1941, the references to 'matt black' were changed, but 'duck egg blue (Sky Type S)' was allowed to stand.

The only explanation ever offered for the use of this term in the past has been that Sky was a new colour and the term 'duck egg blue' was a colloquial descriptive name to give some indication of the actual colour. However, if this is the case, it is odd to say the least that a colour which is so obviously a green should be described as a blue. It will be recalled that when the representatives of the RAE first saw the colour they later named as Sky at Heston, they called it 'Duck Egg Green'.

Perhaps a more likely explanation is that the term 'duck egg blue' was a catch all description pressed into use to describe several slightly different colours, and that 'Sky Type S' was put in brackets to remind everyone that this was the colour which was to be used as and when it became available. Even as late as December, one of the biggest Maintenance Units in the country did not have a Stores Reference Number for Sky, and were apparently issuing Sky Blue for squadrons to apply the new spinner and tail band markings. This will be dealt with in more detail in a later chapter.

When DTD Technical Circular No 144 was issued in March 1941, it cancelled the provisions of all previous DTD Technical Circulars on this subject. In it there is no mention of 'duck egg blue' or 'Sky Type S', but only Sky. By this time, all camouflage colours were supposed to be of Type S and Sky was firmly established in production, so the term 'duck egg blue' which probably referred to BSS 381 (1930) No 1 Sky Blue and or No 16 Eau-de-Nil, was no longer needed. However, the colloquialism 'duck egg blue' lived on in the minds of the general public who were not privy to the official terms and ultimately came to be associated with Sky.

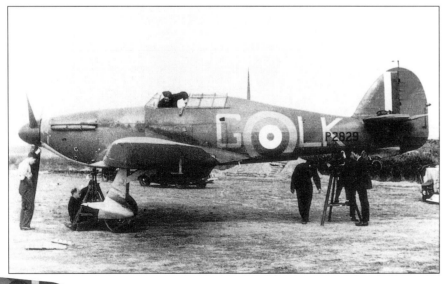

By September 1940, when P2829, LK·G of 87 Sqn was photographed, the manufacturers were starting to apply the correct shade of Sky on the production line. However, as ever, it is virtually impossible to tell whether this aircraft was one of those so coloured.

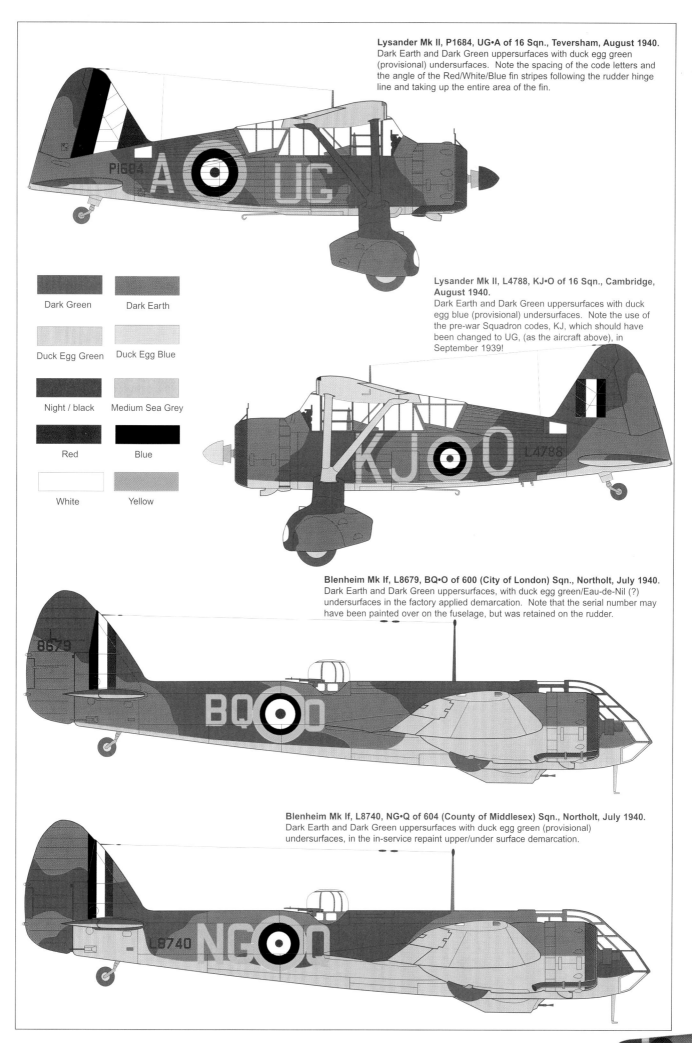

Lysander Mk II, P1684, UG•A of 16 Sqn., Teversham, August 1940.
Dark Earth and Dark Green uppersurfaces with duck egg green (provisional) undersurfaces. Note the spacing of the code letters and the angle of the Red/White/Blue fin stripes following the rudder hinge line and taking up the entire area of the fin.

Dark Green

Dark Earth

Duck Egg Green

Duck Egg Blue

Night / black

Medium Sea Grey

Red

Blue

White

Yellow

Lysander Mk II, L4788, KJ•O of 16 Sqn., Cambridge, August 1940.
Dark Earth and Dark Green uppersurfaces with duck egg blue (provisional) undersurfaces. Note the use of the pre-war Squadron codes, KJ, which should have been changed to UG, (as the aircraft above), in September 1939!

Blenheim Mk If, L8679, BQ•O of 600 (City of London) Sqn., Northolt, July 1940.
Dark Earth and Dark Green uppersurfaces, with duck egg green/Eau-de-Nil (?) undersurfaces in the factory applied demarcation. Note that the serial number may have been painted over on the fuselage, but was retained on the rudder.

Blenheim Mk If, L8740, NG•Q of 604 (County of Middlesex) Sqn., Northolt, July 1940.
Dark Earth and Dark Green uppersurfaces with duck egg green (provisional) undersurfaces, in the in-service repaint upper/under surface demarcation.

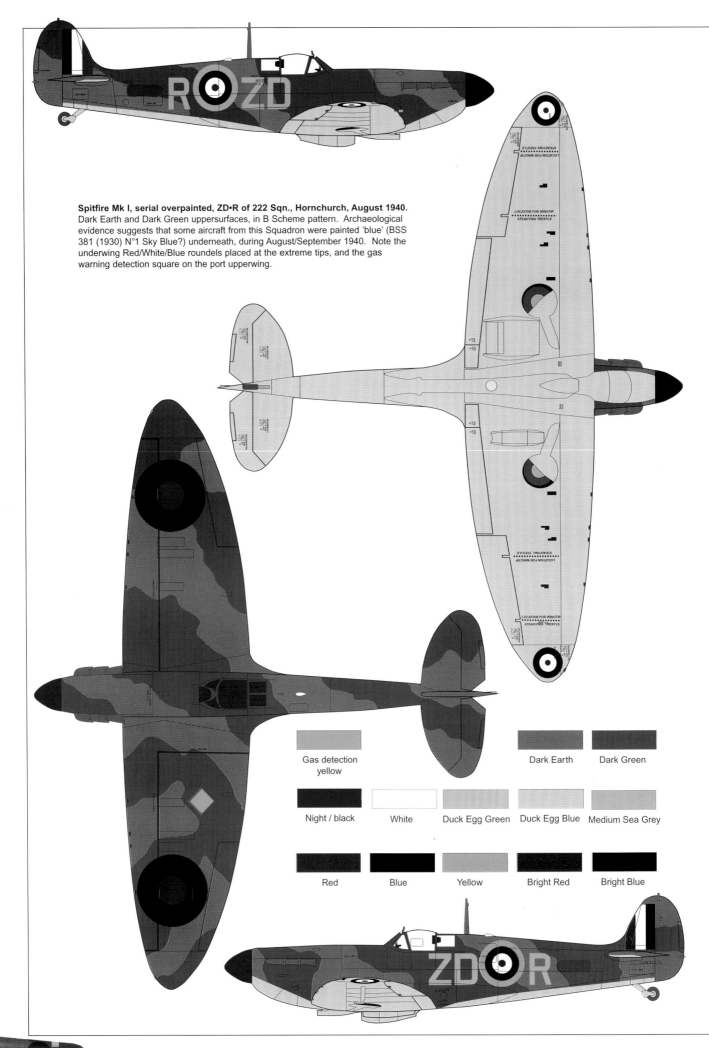

Spitfire Mk I, serial overpainted, ZD•R of 222 Sqn., Hornchurch, August 1940.
Dark Earth and Dark Green uppersurfaces, in B Scheme pattern. Archaeological evidence suggests that some aircraft from this Squadron were painted 'blue' (BSS 381 (1930) N°1 Sky Blue?) underneath, during August/September 1940. Note the underwing Red/White/Blue roundels placed at the extreme tips, and the gas warning detection square on the port upperwing.

Gas detection yellow

Dark Earth

Dark Green

Night / black

White

Duck Egg Green

Duck Egg Blue

Medium Sea Grey

Red

Blue

Yellow

Bright Red

Bright Blue

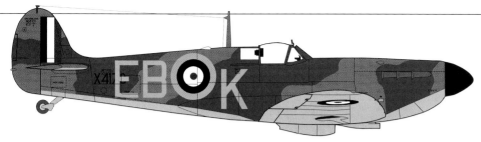

Spitfire Mk I, X4178, EB•K of 41 Sqn., Hornchurch, August 1940.
Dark Earth and Dark Green uppersurfaces, with Sky Grey undersurfaces. N°41 Sqn., was one of the units it is thought that used Sky Grey from the June to late August 1940 period.

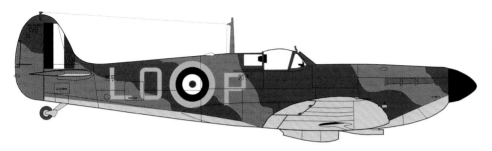

Spitfire Mk I, serial overpainted, LO•P of 602 (City of Glasgow) Sqn., Westhampnett, August 1940.
Dark Earth and Dark Green uppersurfaces, with duck egg green/Eau-de-Nil (?) undersurfaces.

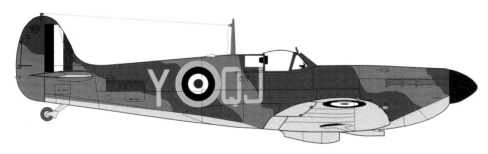

Spitfire Mk I, serial overpainted, QJ•Y of 616 (South Yorkshire) Sqn., Leconfield, August 1940.
Dark Earth and Dark Green uppersurfaces, with 'blue' undersides. N°616 Sqn., are another unit recorded to have used 'blue' undersides during the June to late August 1940 period, which could well have been the pale blue Air Ministry Sky Blue shade, or the duck egg blue BSS 381 (1930) N°1 Sky Blue as illustrated. Note the oversize Red centre to the fuselage roundel thought to be a factory anomaly found on several Spitfires in the mid/late 1940 to late1941 production batch runs.

Hurricane Mk I, P3462, VK•G of 238 Sqn., Middle Wallop, August 1940.
Dark Earth and Dark Green uppersurfaces with duck egg green/Eau-de-Nil (?) undersurfaces. This was a Hawker-built machine. Note how the Yellow outer ring of the fuselage roundel terminates on the upper/under colour demarcation line.

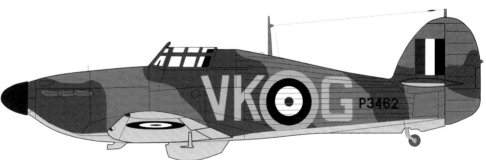

Hurricane Mk I, (P2798 overpainted), LK•A of 87 Sqn., Exeter, August 1940.
Dark Earth and Dark Green uppersurfaces, with duck egg green/Eau-de-Nil (?) undersurfaces. This was a Gloster-built machine, (flown by S/Ldr I R Gleed), and shows the pre-war Bright Red and Bright Blue colours on the fuselage roundel and fin stripes. Upperwing roundels would also have been in Bright colours, although the Squadron or MU applied underwing roundels would have been in the duller wartime Red and Blue. Note the Bright Red spinner.

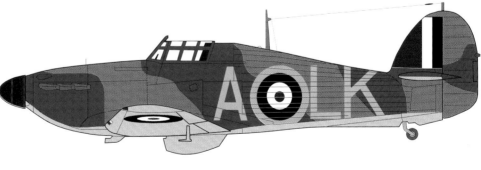

Hurricane Mk I, P3143, NN•D of 310 (Czech) Sqn., Duxford, August 1940.
Dark Earth and Dark Green uppersurfaces with duck egg green/Eau-de-Nil (?) undersurfaces. Another Gloster-built machine, probably with pre-war Bright National markings on the wing uppersurfaces, fuselage sides and fin, with duller wartime colours on the wing undersides.

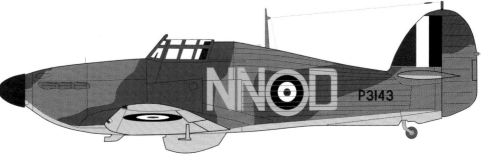

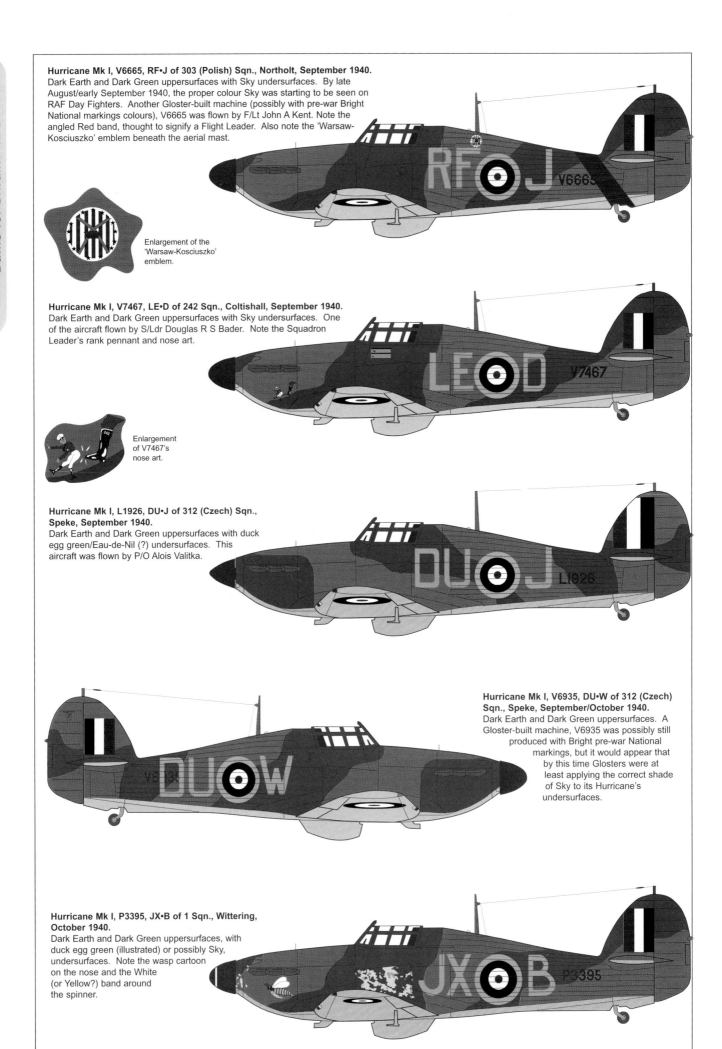

Hurricane Mk I, V6665, RF•J of 303 (Polish) Sqn., Northolt, September 1940.
Dark Earth and Dark Green uppersurfaces with Sky undersurfaces. By late August/early September 1940, the proper colour Sky was starting to be seen on RAF Day Fighters. Another Gloster-built machine (possibly with pre-war Bright National markings colours), V6665 was flown by F/Lt John A Kent. Note the angled Red band, thought to signify a Flight Leader. Also note the 'Warsaw-Kosciuszko' emblem beneath the aerial mast.

Enlargement of the 'Warsaw-Kosciuszko' emblem.

Hurricane Mk I, V7467, LE•D of 242 Sqn., Coltishall, September 1940.
Dark Earth and Dark Green uppersurfaces with Sky undersurfaces. One of the aircraft flown by S/Ldr Douglas R S Bader. Note the Squadron Leader's rank pennant and nose art.

Enlargement of V7467's nose art.

Hurricane Mk I, L1926, DU•J of 312 (Czech) Sqn., Speke, September 1940.
Dark Earth and Dark Green uppersurfaces with duck egg green/Eau-de-Nil (?) undersurfaces. This aircraft was flown by P/O Alois Valitka.

Hurricane Mk I, V6935, DU•W of 312 (Czech) Sqn., Speke, September/October 1940.
Dark Earth and Dark Green uppersurfaces. A Gloster-built machine, V6935 was possibly still produced with Bright pre-war National markings, but it would appear that by this time Glosters were at least applying the correct shade of Sky to its Hurricane's undersurfaces.

Hurricane Mk I, P3395, JX•B of 1 Sqn., Wittering, October 1940.
Dark Earth and Dark Green uppersurfaces, with duck egg green (illustrated) or possibly Sky, undersurfaces. Note the wasp cartoon on the nose and the White (or Yellow?) band around the spinner.

Spitfire Mk I, serial overpainted, YT•F of 65 Sqn., Hornchurch, September 1940.
Dark Earth and Dark Green uppersurfaces with Sky undersurfaces. Note the underwing roundels at the extreme wing tips.

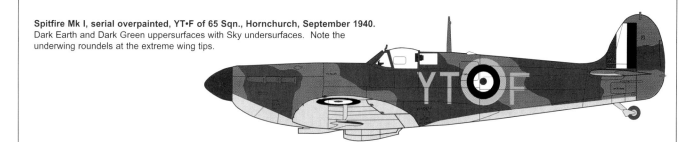

Spitfire Mk I, R6800, LZ•N of 66 Sqn., Gravesend, September 1940.
Dark Earth and Dark Green uppersurfaces with duck egg blue/BS 381 Sky Blue (?) undersurfaces. Flown by S/Ldr R H A Leigh, who, after mistaking his wingman's Spitfire for a Bf 109E, (and spending a nerve-racking few minutes of violent evasive manoeuvres trying to shake him off), ordered all the Squadron's spinners to be painted Red! Note the Medium Sea Grey serial number, and the Squadron Leader's pennant beneath the cockpit windscreen.

Spitfire Mk I, P9386, QV•K of 19 Sqn., Duxford, September 1940.
Dark Earth and Dark Green uppersurfaces with Sky undersurfaces. Flown by S/Ldr Brian Lane, it is thought that the aircraft sported a Yellow propeller spinner.

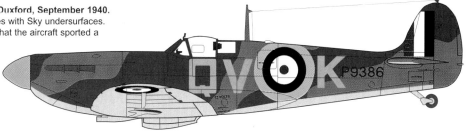

Hurricane Mk I, P3878, YB•W of 17 Sqn., North Weald, September 1940.
Dark Earth and Dark Green uppersurfaces with duck egg green/Eau-de-Nil (?) undersurfaces. Typical of this unit's in-service undersurface re-paints, from June to mid-August 1940, note the irregular demarcation line between the upper and under surface colours on the nose, and the spinner also finished in the undersurface colour. This aircraft was regularly flown by P/O Harold Bird-Wilson.

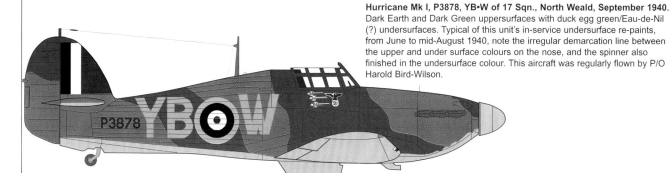

Leading edge of the wing showing the irregular demarcation following the aircraft's in-service re-paint.

Close-up of the artwork carried on P3878's starboard side emergency break-out panel.

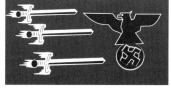

Hurricane Mk I, P3039, RE•D of 229 Sqn., Northolt, September 1940.
Dark Earth and Dark Green uppersurfaces with Sky undersurfaces. P3039 was a Gloster-built machine and would have almost certainly had its National markings in the pre-war Bright colours. This aircraft was flown by P/O 'Vicky' Ortmans. Note the inscription *BéBé* beneath the canopy hood.

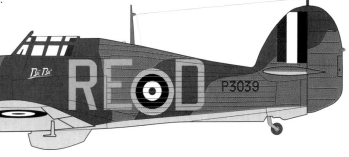

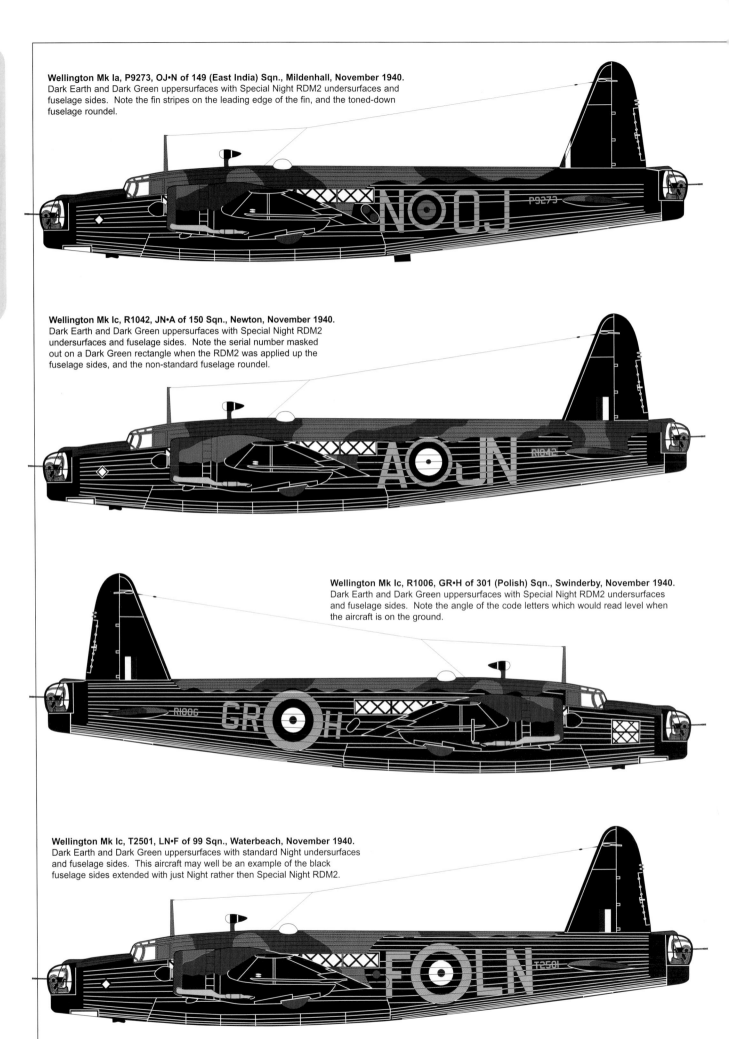

Wellington Mk Ia, P9273, OJ•N of 149 (East India) Sqn., Mildenhall, November 1940.
Dark Earth and Dark Green uppersurfaces with Special Night RDM2 undersurfaces and fuselage sides. Note the fin stripes on the leading edge of the fin, and the toned-down fuselage roundel.

Wellington Mk Ic, R1042, JN•A of 150 Sqn., Newton, November 1940.
Dark Earth and Dark Green uppersurfaces with Special Night RDM2 undersurfaces and fuselage sides. Note the serial number masked out on a Dark Green rectangle when the RDM2 was applied up the fuselage sides, and the non-standard fuselage roundel.

Wellington Mk Ic, R1006, GR•H of 301 (Polish) Sqn., Swinderby, November 1940.
Dark Earth and Dark Green uppersurfaces with Special Night RDM2 undersurfaces and fuselage sides. Note the angle of the code letters which would read level when the aircraft is on the ground.

Wellington Mk Ic, T2501, LN•F of 99 Sqn., Waterbeach, November 1940.
Dark Earth and Dark Green uppersurfaces with standard Night undersurfaces and fuselage sides. This aircraft may well be an example of the black fuselage sides extended with just Night rather then Special Night RDM2.

Wellington Mk Ic, R3209, BU•H of 214 (Federated Malay States) Sqn., Stradishall, November 1940.
Dark Earth and Dark Green uppersurfaces with Special Night RDM2 undersurfaces and fuselage sides.

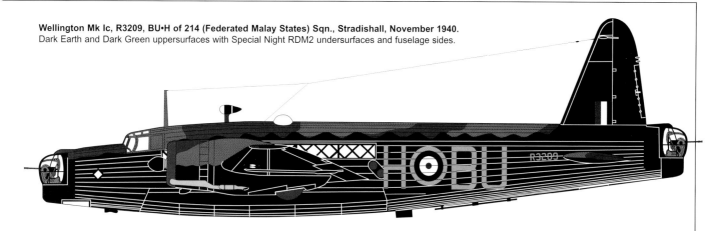

Whitley Mk V, P5004, KN•U of 77 Sqn., Driffield, November 1940.
Dark Earth and Dark Green uppersurfaces with Special Night RDM2 undersurfaces and fuselage sides.

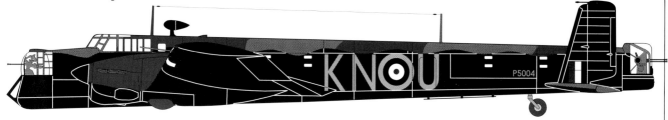

Whitley Mk V, serial overpainted, EY•F of 78 Sqn., Dishforth, November 1940.
Dark Earth and Dark Green uppersurfaces with Special Night RDM2 undersurfaces and fuselage sides. Note the toned-down fuselage roundel and fin stripes.

Whitley Mk V, P5005, DY•N of 102 Sqn., Linton-on-Ouse, November 1940.
Dark Earth and Dark Green uppersurfaces with Special Night RDM2 undersurfaces and fuselage sides. This aircraft was frequently flown by P/O Leonard Cheshire.
Note: When instructions were given for the black finish to be extended up the sides of the fuselage, no directions appear to have been given as to how the serial number was to be presented, consequently each Squadron came up with its own solution. On or about 18 October 1940, Bomber Command instructed that the fuselage serial number should be applied in Red. In view of the difficulty in distinguishing Red from Medium Sea Grey in black and white photographs, all the serials have been illustrated in Medium Sea Grey.

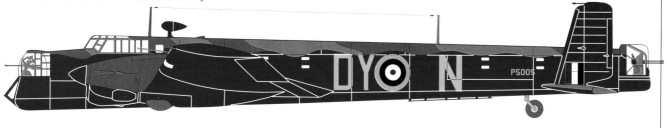

Dark Earth	Dark Green	Night / black	Medium Sea Grey
Red	White	Blue	Yellow

CHAPTER 7
CAMOUFLAGE & MARKING POLICY
Summer 1940

On 23 July 1940, a conference was held at the Air Ministry to consider aircraft colourings and markings with a view to achieving the maximum degree of standardisation. The need for such a conference had been brought about in part by the need to ensure the safety of Allied aircraft by more closely defining the general policy to be adopted regarding the attack by Allied forces of any aircraft of Allied type which was suspected of being flown by the enemy. It was thought preferable that the occasional British or Allied aircraft being flown by the enemy should escape than that instructions should be given which would lead to the destruction of a friendly aircraft in error. No British, Allied, or American type of aircraft was therefore to be regarded as

hostile unless it carried some additional unauthorised marking of a kind which might be useful to the enemy for recognition by his own forces, or unless it acted in an unmistakably hostile manner.

The use of British, European or American aircraft by the Germans was a very real concern to the Air Ministry at this time due to the large numbers of such aircraft which had fallen into German hands as the various European Allied nations on the continent surrendered. The reference to American aircraft appears to have been made as the French had made extensive use of some American types such as the Curtiss Hawk 75 and the outstanding French orders which had not been delivered at the time of the Armistice were in the

process of being diverted to Britain where they would serve alongside American aircraft purchased directly by Britain.

From a production point of view, it was thought necessary to obtain as greater degree of standardisation as possible to ease production and increase output, as well as economising on materials.

Because the various arms of Government had dispersed at the start of the war, the Conference was held at Fisher Road Schools in Harrow, and was attended by representatives from various branches of the Air Ministry, Bomber Command, Fighter Command, Coastal Command, Flying Training Command, Anti-Aircraft Command and the Admiralty.

The first item on the agenda appears

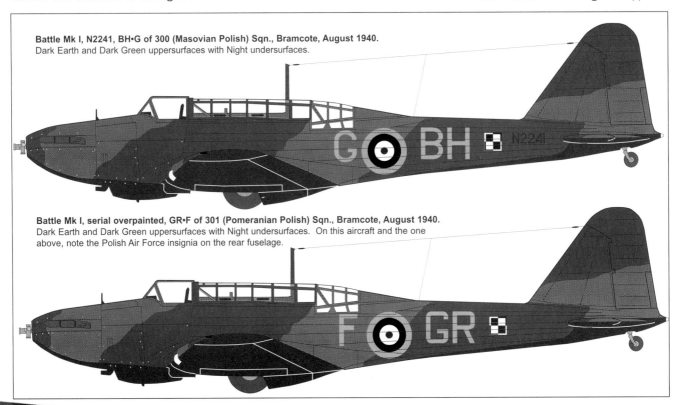

Battle Mk I, N2241, BH·G of 300 (Masovian Polish) Sqn., Bramcote, August 1940.
Dark Earth and Dark Green uppersurfaces with Night undersurfaces.

Battle Mk I, serial overpainted, GR·F of 301 (Pomeranian Polish) Sqn., Bramcote, August 1940.
Dark Earth and Dark Green uppersurfaces with Night undersurfaces. On this aircraft and the one above, note the Polish Air Force insignia on the rear fuselage.

Heading opposite: Hampden, P1333, of 49 Sqn shows the standard bomber finish of mid-1940. Dark Green/Dark Earth uppersurfaces with Night undersurfaces. Red/White/Blue roundels were carried under the wings at this time, a practice which was soon to be abolished. Note the characteristic wavy fuselage demarcation line between the upper and undersurface colours adopted by Handley Page.

Right: With a number of allied air forces having Squadrons within the RAF, (such as Polish, Czech etc), permission was granted for such aircraft that belonged to these Squadrons to carry small national markings. The Polish Air Force national marking can be seen here on the rear fuselage of these 301 (Polish) Sqn Battles, (including P6567, GR·F in the background), photographed at Bramcote circa July/August 1940.

to have been upper surface camouflage. With regard to the upper surfaces, it was agreed that the upper surfaces of all aircraft including target towing and pilotless aircraft should be camouflaged in the Temperate Land Scheme or Temperate Sea Scheme colours, as appropriate to the type of aircraft, and that all aircraft would carry red and blue roundels.

The side surfaces were considered separately and it was decided that the sides of all aircraft except training, communication, and target towing aircraft should be painted in the same colours as the upper surfaces. Training and communications aircraft would remain unaltered, ie they would have the top half painted in the same colours as the upper surfaces and the bottom half painted yellow, whilst target towing aircraft would have the top half of the side surfaces painted in the same colour scheme as the upper surfaces, and the bottom half painted with broad black and yellow diagonal stripes.

Markings on the side surfaces for all aircraft without exception were to be red, white, blue, and yellow roundels with rings of equal size on both sides of the fuselage. All fin surfaces of all aircraft were to carry a red, white, and blue rectangle consisting of three stripes, each of which were to be 8 inches wide with the red stripe leading. This meant that aircraft such as the Hampden would carry flashes on both the inside and outside faces of their twin fins. The rectangle which resulted would therefore be 27 inches high and 24 inches wide, or an area as close to this as the size and shape of the fin would permit. The rectangle was to be based on the lower hinge pin of the rudder.

As has already been mentioned, it was pointed out that two colours being used on the undersurfaces of day flying aircraft, (duck egg blue and silver), to achieve the same effect; and it was decided that duck egg blue (Sky Type S) would replace silver as soon as supplies

Hudsons, such as T9277, QX·W of 224 Sqn., were delivered in a shade of green and brown on the uppersurfaces which were mixed in the USA to match the Air Ministry standards for Dark Green and Dark Earth. Undersurfaces on some aircraft such as this one were silver, on others, they were black.

became available.

There was some discussion on the question of what colour the under surfaces of Searchlight Co-operation Aircraft should be finished in. Anti-Aircraft Commands' representative said that such aircraft should have a conspicuous colour on their under surfaces, but it was pointed out that this would entail disrupting production if this was done by the manufacturers, who in any case would not necessarily know which aircraft would be issued to which units for this purpose. It was therefore agreed that alterations to the standard colour scheme would have to be made locally and that these alterations would take the form of red, white, blue, and yellow roundels with bands of equal width applied to the matt black under surfaces.

Subject to agreement by the War Office, it was decided that pilotless target aircraft should be issued with duck egg blue undersurfaces without roundels and that if necessary, roundels could be painted on by the units themselves.

After some discussion it was agreed that the colour of undersurfaces of operational aircraft should not be rigidly laid down, but that it should be left to the discretion of the Operational Commands as to whether their aircraft were finished in duck egg blue (Sky Type S) or matt black, according to their operational role.

When National markings were considered, Bomber Command's representative explained that Whitleys, which had the lowest casualty rate of all bombers which were employed on the same duties, were finished in matt black without roundels. He therefore asked that the removal of roundels from the undersurfaces of all other aircraft might

be considered. After discussion, it was agreed that roundels would not be carried on the undersurfaces of aircraft with a matt black finish except where the aircraft were tasked with Searchlight Co-operation duties as already mentioned.

For operational day flying aircraft, it was agreed that whilst the Germans continued to carry crosses on their under surfaces, the plain duck egg blue colour scheme without roundels currently in use gave British aircraft a better camouflage effect. At the same time it was thought that the absence of any identification markings at all provided an easy method for the ground defences to distinguish friend from foe. Training, Communication, and Target Towing aircraft would carry red, white, and blue roundels on their under surfaces.

It was ultimately agreed that it was not possible to lay down a permanent and unalterable system of marking. Should the Germans decide to abandon the black crosses they currently carried, then the question of reintroducing roundels on operational aircraft would have to be looked at again.

When the question of code letters was discussed, it was agreed that it would be wrong to use them as a means of recognition. This was because there would always be some aircraft flying without them, such as aircraft being ferried from one place to another. Operational Training Units, which at this time did not carry code letters were to be allotted some as soon as possible to conform with the existing scheme.

With specific points dealt with, the conference then went on to deal with more general issues.

It was agreed that aircraft of Allied Air

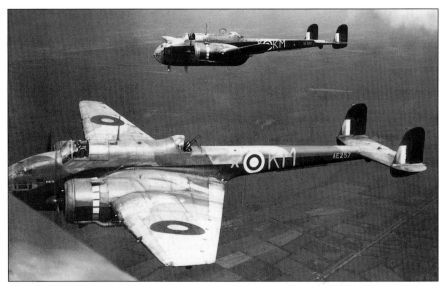

Hampden Mk Is of 44 Sqn with the undersurface matt black Special Night Finish extended up the fuselage sides. Note the fin stripes applied to both the outer and inner faces of the fins. The aircraft in view are AE257, KM·X and AE202, KM·K, photographed over Lincolnshire circa late 1940, (or possibly early 1941), both of which were later lost on operations.

Forces under RAF control must comply with the standard colour and marking schemes as laid down. However, such aircraft were to be allowed to carry small National or squadron markings as long as they were inconspicuous in the air. These badges were to be approved by the Air Ministry in all cases.

The thorny question of the strange colour schemes adopted by aircraft of the PRU was also discussed. Ultimately it was agreed that these aircraft should be excepted from any standard system of colouring and marking. As a consequence of this, it was decided that the PRU would have to make its own arrangements for the safety of its aircraft by keeping the Air Ministry informed of their colour schemes and movements. It was emphasised that whatever colour schemes were adopted, they should not in themselves be regarded as a means of recognition or in any way supersede the National markings.

Given the current concern over the possibility of British aircraft being operated by German crews, it was felt that some guidance should be given over the issue of whether aircraft carrying unauthorised markings should be considered hostile. After some discussion, it was agreed that aircraft carrying additional markings likely to assist the enemy in recognising a British aircraft being flown by a German crew would be sufficient indication of hostility. However, the absence of any authorised British marking could not in itself be regarded as sufficient justification for regarding such an aircraft as hostile.

It was suggested that the possibility of producing coloured illustrations showing the camouflage and markings of British aircraft for the information of all concerned should be looked into.

Finally, it was agreed that the Overseas Commands should not be affected by the rulings given by the conference except that aircraft would be delivered to them with the standard camouflage and markings as used at Home.

The findings and recommendations of this conference were accepted by the Air Ministry and were incorporated into a Camouflage and Markings Policy. The new policy was circulated to all Commands at Home and Overseas, 22 and 61 Groups, the Royal Naval Air Service, the Admiralty, the War Office and Anti-Aircraft Command as well as a large number of departments within the Air Ministry by a letter dated 11 August accompanied by an appendix.

The letter opened by stating that the following matters of policy had been decided upon as a result of a meeting held on 23 July 1940 to consider aircraft camouflage and markings with a view to achieving a maximum degree of standardisation.

The colour schemes and markings which were to be used for different types of aircraft had been standardised as far as possible, and were defined in the attached appendix.

It was decided that since some aircraft might be used for purposes other than those in which they might normally be used, the colour schemes themselves were not to be regarded as a means of recognition for distinguishing friend from foe. Similarly the presence or absence of code letters could not be used as an indication of friendly or hostile character.

As a result, recognition of aircraft by appearance was governed by the constant factors of shape, the presence of red and blue roundels on the upper surfaces of the wings (except on civil aircraft), the presence of red, white and blue stripes on the fin, and the presence of red, white blue and yellow roundels on each side of the fuselage, (again, except on civil aircraft).

It had been found desirable to eliminate roundels from the undersurfaces of all aircraft, but the importance of quick recognition of friendly fighters in a 'dogfight' had led to the adoption of roundels on their undersurfaces.

It was considered inevitable that some period of time would elapse before the new schemes were universally applied. Commands were to inform the Air Ministry when all the aircraft in their Commands had been painted in accordance with the new schemes. Control surfaces were not to be painted pending further instructions regarding special precautions.

Headed 'Secret', the appendix which accompanied the letter was entitled ' Colouring and Marking of British aircraft (Service and Civil)'.
Paragraph 1 gave an explanation of terms.
The Temperate Land Scheme was defined as consisting of two colours Dark Green and Dark Earth.
The Temperate Sea Scheme was defined as consisting of two colours Dark Slate Grey and Extra Dark Sea Grey.
Uppersurfaces were defined as being all the surfaces in plan view as seen from above, including the side surfaces of the fin and rudder. The uppersurfaces of the lower wing and the floats of biplanes and floatplanes were also to be treated as uppersurfaces. The interplane struts of biplanes were to be treated as uppersurfaces, but the struts supporting the floats on seaplanes were to be camouflaged in undersurface colours.
Undersurfaces were the surfaces seen in plan view from below. In the case of biplanes the undersurface of the upper wing was to be treated as an undersurface.

Where two contrasting colours of upper and lower surfaces met, the colours were to be merged into one another, forming no definite line of demarcation. National markings were to be suitably disposed on the defined surfaces as laid down for the individual type and role of the aircraft.

Paragraph 2 set out the requirements for Land Planes except Fleet Air Arm and Civil Aircraft.
Uppersurfaces. The uppersurfaces of all land planes including Target (Pilotless) aircraft were to be camouflaged on the uppersurfaces in the Temperate Land Scheme.

Paragraph 3 dealt with their undersurfaces. The colouring of the undersurfaces were to be as follows.-
(i) Operational aircraft. The undersurfaces of all operational aircraft were to be either matt black or duck egg blue and could be either one or the other at the discretion of individual Commands to meet operational requirements. The following classes of aircraft were to be produced with duck egg blue undersurfaces:- Fighters, Army co-operation, General Reconnaissance, Torpedo bombers, Blenheim bombers, Close support bombers, Troop carriers, and bomber transports. All bombers other than those stated above were to be produced with matt black under surfaces.

Paragraph 4 dealt with Flying Boats, Float Planes, Amphibians, and Fleet Air Arm aircraft.
(i) Upper surfaces. The upper surfaces of

Hawker-built Hurricane Mk I, V7434, DZ·R of 151 Sqn., photographed circa October. This was the finish specified in ADM 332 (Issue 3) which was correct up to and including 8 November 1940.

all Flying Boats, Float Planes, Amphibians, and Fleet Air Arm aircraft were to be camouflaged with the Temperate Sea Scheme with the exception of Target (Pilotless) aircraft whose uppersurfaces were to be camouflaged in the Temperate Land Scheme.

(ii) Undersurfaces. The undersurfaces of all Flying Boats, Float Planes, Amphibians, and Fleet Air Arm aircraft were to be painted duck egg blue.

Paragraph 5 concerned the aircraft of the PRU. These aircraft were to be coloured and marked in accordance with operational requirements, and as a result, the camouflage schemes applied did not need to conform with the standard schemes in use throughout the rest of the RAF. Consequently special arrangements had to be made with Fighter Command Headquarters for the safety of these aircraft.

The next section of the appendix dealt with National markings. Paragraph 7 dealt with those carried by Service aircraft.

(i) Uppersurfaces. Red and blue roundels were carried on the uppersurface of the mainplanes of all service aircraft.

(ii) Sides of Fuselage. A red, white and blue roundel surrounded by a yellow ring was carried on each side of the fuselage of every service aircraft.

(iii). Fin markings. The fin markings were to consist of vertical red, white and blue stripes with the red stripe leading. The stripes were to be 8in wide and 27in high forming a rectangle of 27in by 24in or an area conforming to this as closely as the shape of the fin permitted. The marking was to be placed on the fin against the hinge post immediately above the tailplane.

(iv) Undersurfaces. No roundels were to be carried on the undersurfaces of operational aircraft except fighters, which were to carry red, white and blue roundels. Anti-aircraft (Searchlight) Co-operation aircraft were to carry red, white and blue roundels surrounded by a yellow ring. Target (pilotless) aircraft could carry

roundels at the discretion of the unit commander for training purposes. Paragraph 8 dealt with other markings carried by Service aircraft, such as Registration Numbers (serial numbers), Code Letters, and Special Markings, for which it was stated that no special markings were to be carried except by aircraft of Allied Air Forces operating under RAF control, or where it was desired to distinguish particular or presentation aircraft. In such cases a marking not larger than 9 inches by 6 inches or an inscription in 2 inch grey letters could be applied to the fuselage forward of the trailing edge of the wing providing permission was given by the Command Headquarters concerned.

The text of this appendix was circulated in full as part of DTD Technical Circular No 83 on 23 August 1940.

Chemical Warfare

One area of markings policy about which little is currently known, is that which relates to chemical warfare. During the summer of 1940, many types of aircraft carried small squares of a light greenish yellow gas detection paint. Sometimes this was painted directly onto the aircraft, and on others it seems to have taken the form of a square of fabric treated with gas detection paint which was doped onto the aircraft using a thin border of fabric treated with the red primer to hold it in place.

By September 1940, the RAF had eleven Bomber and several Army Co-operation squadrons equipped with Mustard gas bombs and/or spraying equipment, which was intended to be used in retaliation should the Germans resort to the use of such weapons during an invasion. It is presumed that the gas detection markings were applied to British aircraft as an indicator for the ground crew that the aircraft had been contaminated whilst operating in a chemical warfare environment.

Fortunately this never happened, and the markings seem to have disappeared by the spring of 1941.

Gas Detection panels were quite a common sight on RAF aircraft during 1940. Here they are seen on the wheel spat of Lysander L4818, KO·L of 2 Sqn., (above), which was one of the Squadrons which would have been tasked with delivering Mustard Gas by aerial spraying had invasion happened; and this Spitfire of 616 Sqn., (opposite), serial unknown but coded QJ·X, which may have been called upon to operate in a contaminated area.

CHAPTER 8
AT THE SHARP END

September - December 1940

Whilst the Air Ministry was busily formulating new policy, the Ministry of Aircraft Production was trying to put the existing policy into effect. Despite the fact that the pre-war Bright Red and Bright Blue colours were supposed to have been dropped from camouflaged aircraft some two or three years previously, it would appear that not all aircraft manufacturers had grasped this fact, or alternatively had large stocks of these colours which they wished to use up.

On 1 September 1940, the MAP sent a circular to all the RTOs with reference to DTD Technical Circular No 84 'Identification Colours on Aircraft'. The RTOs were to advise their companies that dull identification colours were required for the National markings on aircraft. The reminder was necessary because it would appear that several companies were still purchasing, (or at least using), the pre-war colours which were glossy and bright.

Archaeological evidence shows that one of the offending firms using the pre-war Bright Red and Bright Blue in the National markings which were being applied to new production aircraft at about this time, was Glosters who were involved in the production of Hurricanes.

The remains of Hurricane Mk I,

R4116 of 615 Sqn which was lost on 28 August held at Kent Battle of Britain Museum at Hawkinge, shows the pre-war Bright Red and Bright Blue to be still being applied to Gloster-built Hurricanes to advantage.

From this it is possible to infer that all previous Hurricanes built by this company left the production line with National markings applied in the pre-war bright colours. However there is some evidence to suggest that this fault was corrected to some extent, either by the MUs before

issue, or by the squadrons themselves. Other aircraft known to have been finished with these colours from earlier production batches are Hurricanes P2728 and P3049, the remains of which both show clear evidence of having the Bright Blue overpainted with the wartime dull shade, simply termed Blue, at some point prior to their loss.

The photographs of the fuselage roundel taken from an unidentified Hurricane of 303 Sqn which was lost on 27 September, and reproduced in

Heading: Blenheim Mk IV, R3600, VE·H of 110 Sqn. This aircraft had its code letters applied in Medium Sea Grey and its individual aircraft letter applied in white. Built by Rootes between March/June 1940, this aircraft has a duck egg green colour, similar to BSS 381 (1930) No 16 Eau-de-Nil, on its undersurfaces.

Right: Two Gloster-built Hurricanes, R4218, UF·U of 601 Sqn., (above) and P3039 RE·D of 229 Sqn., (opposite) both of which appear to display the use of the pre-war bright red and bright blue colours on the fuselage roundels and fin stripes.

When the Special Night finish was extended up the fuselage sides and over the fins of Night Bombers in September 1940, Squadrons found that it did not adhere to the aircraft as well as it should. This particular Whitley Mk V, P4938, KN·C of 77 Sqn., shows distinct signs of peeling along the leading edges of the tail fins.

photographs 9 and 10 on the inside back cover, illustrate the difference in the colours. The Bright Red of the centre spot contrasts quite well with the dull red finish of the red dope used to tauten the fabric which was almost identical to the correct identification colour, again simply termed, Red. The difference between Bright Blue and Blue is less easy to make out but is nonetheless real. At first glance it appeared that the Bright Blue segment of the roundel was dirty, but upon closer examination, it became clear that the Bright Blue had been over painted with Blue at some point. It did not appear that the Bright Red centre had been over painted with Red.

This artefact also gave a very clear indication of how the roundels were applied on the production line. Careful examination of the Bright Red centre spot will reveal a small hole made by the pair of compasses used to mark out the roundel. This appears to have been applied in two stages. First, the White and Yellow disks were marked out, painted in and left to dry. The Bright Red centre and Bright Blue ring were then applied over the top to give the full four colour roundel.

It is not known when, (or if), Glosters ceased to use the Bright Red and Bright Blue colours, nor, unfortunately, is it known who the other guilty parties were. There must have been several, otherwise a circular would not have been sent.

There were also problems with the application of camouflage finishes. Over the first six months of 1940 Special Night to DTD Specification RDM2 was put into large scale production and began to be applied to Armstrong Whitworth Whitleys on the production line. Problems were not long in coming though, as on 24 July, Armstrong Whitworth at Coventry sent a Postagram to the RAE outlining the problems the Company was having in applying this finish to the Whitleys then being produced. Upon application to the aircraft, the Special Night attacked the Primer and both finishes peeled off in big flakes!

With all the problems which were being encountered with this finish, a member of staff from the RAE was despatched to Coventry to examine the problem at the end of July. Initially, it appeared that the problem lay in the thinners with which the manufacturers were thinning both the Special Night and Primer. This was apparently old stock of poor quality and with other users also

No precise instructions were given as to exactly how the Special Night finish was to be extended up the fuselage sides. This resulted in many variations between Squadrons. Compare the finish on these two Wellingtons, L7788, KX·E of 311 (Czech) Sqn., (above), and AA·Y of 75 Sqn (opposite).

reporting problems with the Special Night, it was decided that the answer lay in revising the chemical formula using a more volatile chemical base.

From early September the use of this finish was extended up the sides of all night bombers so that only the top quarter of the fuselage remained in the disruptive camouflage scheme, and over the fin and rudder. Here too problems with applying the finish were encountered with the new finish cracking and peeling away after only a very short time. The worst problems seemed to lie in trying to apply it to metal, as it was found that it took to the fabric parts of the Wellington much more readily than the metal parts.

After some experimentation, by the end of September, the formula had been radically revised to contain Ethyl Cellulose and the nomenclature of the specification for Special Night was changed from RDM2 to RDM2A. The new specification Special Night was included in AP 1086 the Vocabulary of Stores as 33B/375. Its Thinner was 33B/340.

Whilst the use of this finish was regarded as highly secret, the cat had in fact got out of the bag. On 31 August 1940, the New York Times reported that the British had perfected some form of secret varnish which rendered their aircraft virtually invisible at night even in the most powerful searchlights! This report appears to have been based on information received from Germany which might suggest that making the aircraft *virtually invisible* was not quite good enough.

Even in Britain, every schoolboy who

When Coastal Command began to debate the colour which was to be applied to the undersurfaces of its operational landplanes, the Blenheim Day Fighter Squadrons wished to remain in their day flying colours as they were not required to operate at night. The continuing use of the Day Fighter finish is shown on this Blenheim IVf, P6957, LA·R of 235 Sqn., circa September 1940.

had a copy of the 1940 edition of 'Aircraft of the Fighting Powers' was in on the secret to a limited extent, as the book noted that "....certain Wellingtons are now painted with a special anti-searchlight paint...."; whilst Whitleys also carried what is described as "....the new camouflage paint to defeat searchlights...." but "....no details can be revealed....".

As no directions appear to have been given as to how the fuselage serial number, which up until this time had been applied in Night, was to be applied following the instruction to extend the Special Night finish up the fuselage sides, each squadron came up with its own solution. Some squadrons painted around it, leaving the original Night marking on a background of Dark Green and/or Dark Earth, whilst others re-applied the markings over the Special Night finish using either Medium Sea Grey or Red. Finally, on or about 18 October, Bomber Command instructed that the fuselage serial number should be applied in Red paint.

Coastal Command was meanwhile wrestling with the contradictory camouflage requirements of aircraft which were required to fly both by day and by night. On 11 September, HQ Coastal Command wrote to all its Groups stating that as the operational landplanes in the Command were employed on both day and night flying, it was difficult to discriminate which individual aircraft should have their undersurfaces painted black and which should be duck egg blue. It had therefore been decided that all landplane undersurfaces should be painted matt black with no roundels.

This did not prove popular at squadron level, and requests were made that some aircraft be allowed to continue to be finished with duck egg blue undersurfaces for use in daylight. On 16

October HQ 16 Group wrote to HQ Coastal Command to inform them that 235 Sqn equipped with Blenheim Day Fighters had signalled 16 Group to say that their undersurfaces should be duck egg blue due to the fact that they were not required to operate at night. Similarly 206 Sqn, equipped with Hudsons were expected to carry out frequent convoy escort work by day as well as by night. They therefore requested that a small number of their Hudsons should remain painted duck egg blue. HQ 16 Group considered that this was a reasonable request, and stated that pending authority from HQ Coastal Command, they had granted permission for this to be so.

At this point in the proceedings a conference appears to have been held at HQ Coastal Command to discuss in detail the camouflage requirements of the Command. As a result, the following colour schemes were decided upon.
General Reconnaissance and Torpedo Bomber landplanes.
Uppersurfaces - Temperate Land Scheme
Undersurfaces - Up to 25 percent of aircraft in duck egg blue, the remainder matt black.
Nos 53 and 59 Squadrons (equipped with Blenheim IV bombers)
Uppersurfaces - Temperate Land Scheme
Undersurfaces - Matt black.
Long range fighter squadrons
Uppersurfaces - Temperate Land Scheme
Undersurfaces - Duck egg blue
Flying boats
Uppersurfaces - Temperate Sea Scheme
Undersurfaces - To be left bare of any

colouring, and protected by a coat of clear Lanolin to prevent corrosion.

These decisions were sent out to the operational Groups in a letter dated 8 November.

The decision to leave the undersurfaces of flying boats unpainted and protected with a coat of clear Lanolin was contrary to the then current Air Ministry scheme which called for all flying boats to be finished duck egg blue underneath. On 2 December HQ 17 Group informed HQ Coastal Command that Calshot had reported that the contractor was delivering Saro Lerwick flying boats with duck egg blue undersurfaces, and sought guidance as to whether this should be removed. This seems to have drawn the current Air Ministry schemes to the attention of Coastal Command which evidently then had a rethink on this point. With Sky pigmented Lanolin just starting to become available, to DTD 420, on 6 December HQ Coastal Command informed 17 Group that Lerwicks were to be left in the duck egg blue finish.

During October 1940, the *Luftwaffe* switched its tactics and heavily increased the strength of its night raids at the expense of ceasing its massed daylight raids almost all together. Such daylight raids that did take place, almost entirely consisted of fighters and fighter-bombers operating at comparatively high speed and altitude. This change in tactics caused the British a number of problems.

The daylight fighter-bomber raids caused problems because the Chain Home radars then in service had great difficulty in tracking targets either at great altitude or low level. When the targets were moving at high speed as well, the problem was compounded. Part of the solution to this was the formation of 421 Flight which flew standing patrols at high altitude to try to visually acquire incoming raids and then report their position until an interception was made. However, with the fighting now taking place at a greater speed and altitude than previously, the

No 206 Sqn., equipped with Hudsons, also protested at the decision to paint all Coastal Command landplane undersurfaces matt black. However, as they flew by day *and* by night, they requested that a small number of their aircraft should remain in the day flying colours. T9303, VX·V, was one of the aircraft painted with matt black undersides.

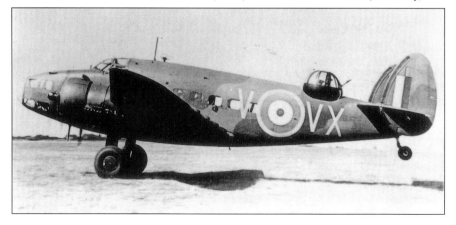

When Sky was introduced on Day Fighter undersurfaces in June 1940, underwing roundels were also abolished. However, the importance of quick recognition of friendly fighters in combat led to the re-introduction of underwing roundels in mid-August. This Hurricane Mk I, V6632, UF•L of 601 Sqn., was photographed at Exeter in late 1940 and shows, (possibly 45 inch diameter), underwing roundels and either Eau-de-Nil or Sky undersurfaces. (via Michael Payne)

colour schemes of British fighters began to cause problems.

The first of these was one of identification. Without a firm radar track, valuable time could be spent either trying to intercept, or avoid, friendly aircraft, and it was apparently felt that the identification markings should be made more prominent. On 22 October 1940 the Air Ministry signalled HQ Coastal Command to inform them that HQ Fighter Command had suggested that the identification markings for fighter aircraft should be changed, seeking HQ Coastal Command's opinion.

The changes were to consist of re-introducing the half black and half white special identification marking on the undersides, with red, white, and blue roundels, the roundel on the black wing having a yellow surround; and introducing a duck egg blue spinner, along with a duck egg blue tail band, some 18 inches in width, immediately in front of the tailplane and which was to run right around the fuselage.

An internal Coastal Command Memo shows that this Command was not impressed with the idea of re-introducing the special identification marking. Whilst it was not a problem, "if you live under the umbrella", it was "a different proposition when over enemy territory or over ships at sea". This marking was thought to make the aircraft *too* conspicuous.

The *Luftwaffe's* switch to night bombing caused problems because the fighter force which had successfully defended Britain in daylight was for the most part ineffective at night. This was not entirely unexpected as specialised Night Fighters, equipped with airborne radar, such as the Beaufighter were under development, but until such time as both they and the new Ground Controlled Interception radar could be made to work properly, Britain's night defences would have a thin time of it. The

emergence of specialised Night Fighters raised the question of what camouflage it would be most effective for them to adopt.

The questions of fighter camouflage and markings were addressed at a meeting held at the Air Ministry on 30 October 1940.

Fighter Command's representative outlined the Command's proposal to re-introduce the black and white markings, and to introduce the new tail band and spinner markings. The changes of colouring and marking of fighter aircraft since they had last carried the Night and White undersurfaces were reviewed, and it was pointed out that it had been decided as a matter of principle that colour schemes in themselves were not to be regarded as a means of telling friend from foe. It was also pointed out that if frequent alterations were to be made in camouflage and markings for operational reasons, then it was best that they should be made by either the ASUs or the squadrons themselves in order to avoid upsetting production.

The Fighter Command representative explained that the need for change was founded in the necessity of enabling British fighters to distinguish other British fighters flying above them and thus avoid being surprised by enemy aircraft.

After some discussion it was decided that it would suffice for the port wing to be painted black using the new DTD 441 distemper. It was also agreed that a yellow ring should be added to the roundel under the black port wing, and that the spinner and tail band markings

should be adopted, but that these markings would only apply to fighters in Fighter Command. Fighters belonging to Commands such as Coastal Command would not be affected.

The camouflage of Night Fighters was then considered. It was subsequently agreed that Night Fighters would be coloured black all over and would be marked in an identical manner to Night Bombers.

All fighters except Boulton Paul Defiants, Douglas DB 7 fighters and Bristol Beaufighters would continue to be produced in the same colours as at present, ie the Temperate Land Scheme on the upper surfaces and what the minutes of the meeting described as "Sky Type S blue" on the under surfaces. Defiants and DB 7 fighters only were to be produced coloured black all over, whilst Beaufighters were to be delivered finished in primer only and were then to be finished in an appropriate scheme for their role by the ASUs.

Fighter aircraft already in service which were being used operationally at night were to be coloured black by Fighter Command units. Replacement aircraft were to be coloured black by the ASUs before issue.

The black to be used was described in the minutes as "special night flying black dope", which would appear to mean Special Night.

Finally, Fighter Command's representative requested that the aircraft of 421 Flight should be allowed the same freedom regarding colour schemes as was already allowed to the PRU. This was agreed.

All concerned with the introduction of the new Special Night finish appear to have been informed of the change from the Day Fighter scheme on 11 November.

With the extension of the Special Night finish on bombers and the new requirements for Night Fighters, a shortage of Special Night ensued. To some extent this was alleviated by the

Spitfire X4389, LO•G of 602 Sqn., shows the standard Day Fighter finish as it was at the end of September. However, the identification markings it carried were found to be inadequate during the combats at higher altitudes which took place from October onwards.

decision to first of all apply a coat of Night to serve as an undercoat before Special Night was used as a final finishing coat.

On 27 November, HQ 41 Group sent a Postagram to the Air Ministry to voice its concern over the decision that Beaufighters should be finished in primer only before delivery. It was stated that Beaufighters did not come from the contractors to 41 Group direct at that time, but went via either 30 MU or 32 MU under 43 Group in order to have various items of equipment, such as their airborne radar for Fighter Command, or their navigation equipment for Coastal Command, fitted. The Postagram then went on to point out that even when the aircraft had arrived at ASUs it might not be possible to apply the camouflage finish straight away, and in the meantime, the aircraft would be stored out in the open thus rendering them liable to corrosion.

41 Group strongly recommended that Beaufighters continued to be delivered from the contractors in the existing camouflage with a light blue undersurface pending a decision by Coastal Command on their requirements in cockpit and signals layout. Once this had been decided, then it might prove possible to determine the eventual role of the aircraft at an early stage in its life, and thus apply the appropriate camouflage on the production line.

These recommendations led to the idea of delivering Beaufighters in only their primer finish being dropped on 5 December with instructions being passed to resume deliveries in the Temperate Land and duck egg blue scheme.

As was usual it took some time for this change in policy to work its way through the system as on 28 December, 252 Squadron complained to HQ Coastal Command that it had just taken delivery of two Beaufighters, R2198 and R2199, which were uncamouflaged, and still in their primer finish. The Squadron was not happy about this and requested that future deliveries would be already camouflaged as they did not have the facilities to do this kind of work within the Squadron.

The changes in the colouring of the Day Fighter force began on 27 November 1940, when signal X789 notified Commands that the undersurface of the port wing on Day Fighters in Fighter Command were to be painted black, and the roundel on this surface was once again to be surrounded by a Yellow ring. New markings were also to be applied in the form of a vertical duck egg blue band, 18 inches wide, which was to be painted completely around the fuselage immediately in front of the tailplane, and the spinner was to be completely painted in duck egg blue. Night Fighters were to be painted black on all surfaces and to carry national markings as for Night Bombers.

The following day, Signal X338 made reference to Signal X798 and stated that Fighter Command units were to suspend action on altering the colour scheme of their aircraft until they received an executive order from HQ Fighter Command but were to obtain the necessary materials necessary to carry out the alterations at short notice.

Signal A131 of 2 December referred to X789 of 27 November and X338 of 28 November and went on to say that it was understood that several units had already completed painting the new markings on their aircraft, and that such markings were to remain as permission was now given for all units to proceed in accordance with the provisions of X789 of 27 November. As, over the next few days, fighters would be seen in both the old and the new markings, units were advised that special care should be exercised in identification to avoid mistakes in recognition occurring.

As units began to apply for stores for supplies of paint to apply the new spinner and tail band markings, No 3 MU at Milton signalled the RAE on 18 December advising them that No 3 MU had no Vocabulary of Stores reference number for Sky. The RAE was invited to inform the MU exactly which shade of Sky, Blue or Grey was required!

They then stated that they were issuing 33B/191 which was Dark Earth, and 33B/262 which was a light grey primer. As this makes no sense in this context, it is thought likely that 33B/191 is some kind of typing error. Examination of the available Stores Reference numbers reveals that if 33B/191 *is* an error, the most likely number for it to be given in error of, is 33B/291. 33B/291 was Sky Blue to DTD 314 in a one gallon container.

Given that there are eyewitness accounts of both light grey and light blue spinners and tail bands during this period, and many black and white photographs clearly show a marked difference in tone between the newly painted spinner and tail band, and the existing undersurfaces, this might well be the reason. It would therefore appear that many aircraft had 33B/291 Sky Blue spinners and tail bands.

Exactly how widespread this was is not known, but it is thought that Sky Blue spinners and tail bands only began to die out with the introduction of the Day Fighter Scheme in the summer of 1941. Up until this time it would appear that the painting of the spinners and tail bands was carried out by the ASUs or squadrons themselves, and not by the contractors. When the contractors did take over the responsibility for applying these markings, they would appear to have correctly used Sky.

One further change seems to have been brought about by the switch in *Luftwaffe* tactics. From October onwards, Day Fighter pilots began to report that the camouflage finish applied to their fighters appeared to be too dark for use at the altitudes at which they were now flying. As a result of this, much experimental work was to be done during 1941 which led ultimately to the adoption of the Day Fighter Scheme. In the interim there is a small body of evidence to suggest that the uppersurface camouflage of some Spitfire Mk IIs, built at Castle Bromwich, *might* have had their uppersurface camouflage 'lightened' by the use of Light Earth in place of Dark Earth. This however remains unconfirmed at the time of writing.

Fighter Command's solution to the identification problem was to introduce a black finish under the port wing and a 'duck egg blue' spinner and 18 inch wide tail band. Hurricane V7462, JU•T of 111 Sqn., illustrates the contrast between the colour of the spinner and tail band and the undersurfaces.

Hurricane Mk I, P3682, DX•L of 245 Sqn., Aldergrove, October 1940.
Dark Earth and Dark Green uppersurfaces with Sky undersurfaces.
Even as late as October 1940, aircraft were still to be seen with non-standard, narrow Yellow outlines to the fuselage roundels as this illustrations shows.

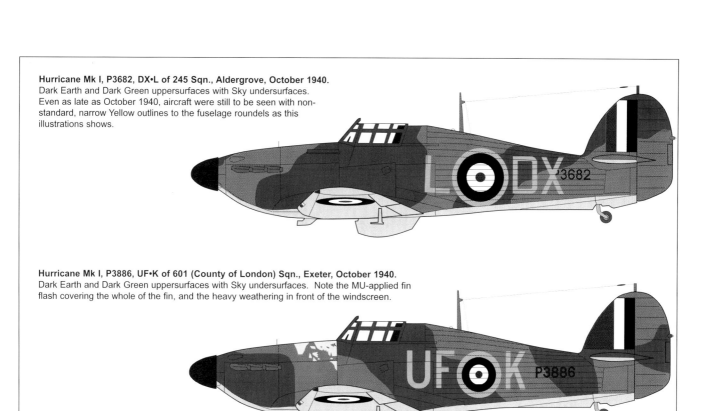

Hurricane Mk I, P3886, UF•K of 601 (County of London) Sqn., Exeter, October 1940.
Dark Earth and Dark Green uppersurfaces with Sky undersurfaces. Note the MU-applied fin flash covering the whole of the fin, and the heavy weathering in front of the windscreen.

Blenheim Mk IV, N3537, TR•J of 59 Sqn., Thorney Island, October 1940.
Dark Earth and Dark Green uppersurfaces with Night undersurfaces. Being part of Coastal Command, most of N°59 Sqn's bomber Blenheims followed the decision to paint all Coastal Command's landplane undersurfaces matt black, as here in N3537's case.

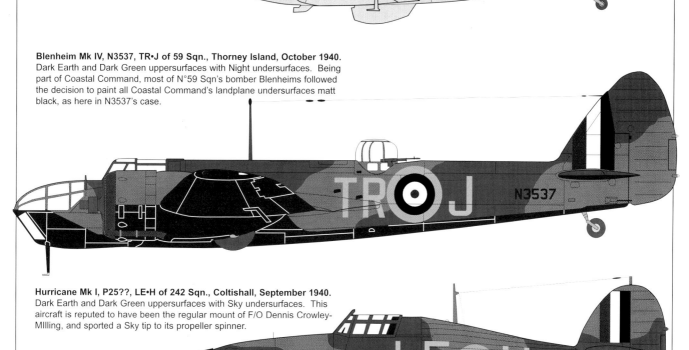

Hurricane Mk I, P25??, LE•H of 242 Sqn., Coltishall, September 1940.
Dark Earth and Dark Green uppersurfaces with Sky undersurfaces. This aircraft is reputed to have been the regular mount of F/O Dennis Crowley-MIlling, and sported a Sky tip to its propeller spinner.

Hurricane Mk I, R4175, RF•R of 303 (Polish) Sqn., Northolt, September 1940.
Dark Earth and Dark Green uppersurfaces with Sky undersurfaces. Another Gloster-built aircraft with pre-war Bright National markings, R4175 was regularly flown by Sgt Josef Frantisek who claimed at least seven 'kills' using this machine.

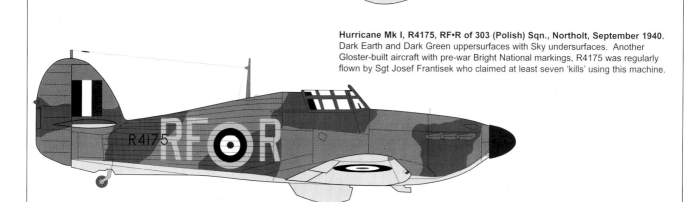

CHAPTER 9
CONSOLIDATION
November - December 1940

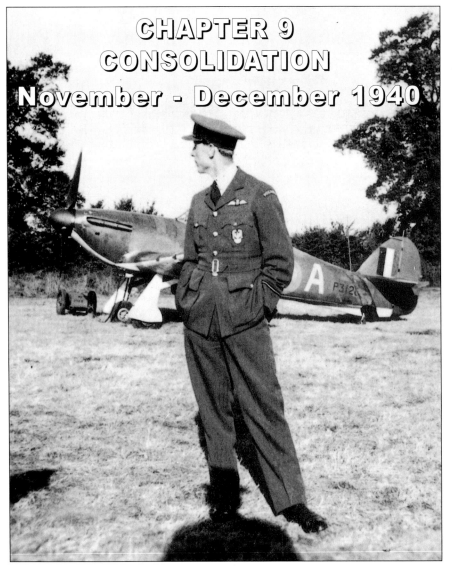

With all the changes and revisions in specifications brought about during 1940, by November the camouflage and markings requirements for RAF aircraft were scattered about in many different documents, each of which had a different distribution list. As a consequence confusion very often reigned at all levels. The first step in attempting to bring some order to the subject was to revise Aircraft Design Memorandum 332.

Therefore, on 15 November 1940, Aircraft Design Memorandum No 332 (Issue 3) 'External Colour Schemes of Aircraft' was issued. It began by stating that this ADM concerned the external colour schemes of aircraft, but not airscrews which were to be finished as required by the relevant airscrew specifications.

The design of the camouflage or other external colour scheme was to be in accordance with the appropriate Air Diagram,. All had been revised to incorporate the 'ad hoc' instructions

Examples of unauthorised markings on a pair of 303 (Polish) Squadron Hurricane Mk Is. P3128, RF·A (above) shows what appears to be an angled *blue* band on the rear fuselage in front of the tailplane, whilst V6665, RF·J (opposite), appears to have a *red* band in a similar position. It has been suggested that these bands were applied to (A and B?) Flight Commanders' aircraft. (via Michael Payne)

contained in DTD Technical Circular letters AMO(A)s and Postagrams issued upto and including 8 November 1940. Where reference was made to Specifications, or Air Diagrams, the use of the latest issue was implied.

New types of aircraft, the outline shape of which were not generally known to the Services were to be finished to the nearest 'Trainer' or 'Communication' scheme. This applied to aircraft of a purely experimental type and also to new design prototypes of a production design delivered for DTD trials prior to the date when deliveries to normal RAF units

began.

Where any of the Air Diagrams showed two variations of the scheme, (ie the mirror images of one another), the variations were to be allocated to aircraft as directed in the contract instructions.

Each of these Air Diagrams illustrated the general requirements for each class of aircraft, and manufacturers had to adapt these designs to the design proposed for specific types, the resulting design having to be approved by the DTD. These works drawings were to be fully dimensioned and specify which materials were to be used on metal and wood parts. Exhaust stub pipes and manifolds were not to be painted.

Under the heading of miscellaneous types were Night Fighters, Ambulance aircraft, and Captured enemy aircraft. Night Fighters were to be camouflaged the same way as Day Fighters. Captured enemy aircraft were to be camouflaged in the appropriate 'Communications' scheme.

Dry spraying was to be avoided and as smooth a finish as possible was to be obtained. Where the contrasting colours of the upper and lower surfaces met, the colours were to be merged into one another forming no definite line of demarcation by merging the colour of the uppersurface downwards into the undersurface colour. Any camouflaged parts to be delivered to Stores, or spares were to have their external surfaces treated with the appropriate primer or red dope only

Whilst this document served to inform the contractors of the colour schemes which they were supposed to apply on the production line, the Service users of the aircraft were brought as fully upto date as possible with the issue of AMO A.926 - 'Aircraft Colouring and Recognition Markings' on 12 December 1940. Being a slightly later document than ADM 332 Issue 3, the AMO was more up to date, incorporating the changes which had come about after 8 November.

This AMO superseded all the previous instructions on this subject as given in AMOs A.154/39, A.298/39 and A.520/39, and was split into two sections. Section I dealt with aircraft camouflage, and Section II aircraft

A well-known but none-the-less interesting photograph of a Castle Bromwich-built Spitfire Mk II, P7666, EB·Z of 41 Sqn., in late 1940 finish. Of particular interest is the obvious difference in colour between the spinner and tail band, thought to have been applied in Sky Blue, and the undersurfaces which were Sky. By this time, Type S materials seem to have been in common use as indicated by the overall sheen of the aircraft which is especially noticeable on the tailplane.

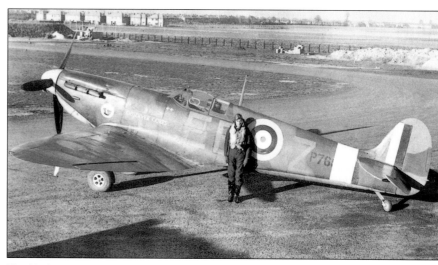

markings. The regulations contained therein were to apply to all RAF aircraft at home and overseas but could be varied to meet operational requirements at the discretion of Air Officers Commanding Overseas Commands with Air Ministry approval.

Section I was entitled 'Camouflage Colouring of British Aircraft, including American and Allied Types in use by British Air Forces' and began with an explanation of terms.

The Temperate Land Scheme camouflage was defined as being two colours, Dark Green and Dark Earth. Aircraft of the Middle East Command were to be coloured Midstone in place of the Dark Green.

The Temperate Sea Scheme camouflage was defined as being two colours, Dark Grey (sic) and Extra Dark Sea Grey. (Dark Grey was presumably a misprint for Dark Slate Grey as this error was later corrected by AMO A.30 dated 9 January 1941.

With these definitions established, the Order then went on to describe the camouflage schemes of landplanes except Fleet Air Arm aircraft, (as described in Chapter 7). The only real changes concerned the undersurfaces of operational aircraft, which were still to be either matt black or duck egg blue at the discretion of Commands to meet operational requirements, but included the the following amendments.

The following classes of aircraft are to be produced with duck egg blue (Sky Type S) under surfaces:- Day Fighters, Blenheim bombers, Army C-operation types, Close support bombers, General Reconnaissance aircraft, Troop carriers, Torpedo bombers, and Bomber transports. Day Fighters are to be coloured black on the under surface of the port wing by Aircraft Storage Units before delivery to Fighter Command units.

All bombers except those referred to above are to be produced with matt black undersurfaces. The black covering is to be extended to include the side surfaces of the fins and rudders. Furthermore, on bomber aircraft the undersurfaces are to be interpreted as including the side surfaces up to the outline of the top quarter of of the fuselage cross section.

Hurricane Mk I of 605 Sqn, (serial unknown), coded UP·U, photographed wearing the then new spinner and tail band marking formerly promulgated by AMO A.926 of 12 December 1940. These identification markings were applied at Squadron and/or MU level until well into 1941, which may account for the overpainting of the serial number and the noted variations in their colour.

The National markings on these surfaces are to be left unchanged and not obscured by the matt black finish.

Operational aircraft temporarily on the strength of experimental establishments for short periods of time are allowed to retain their operational colouring. The under surfaces of Flying Boats, Floatplanes, Amphibians and Fleet Air Arm aircraft are to be duck egg blue (Sky Type S).

Finally in the camouflage section, the Order outlined the camouflage schemes carried by aircraft of the Photographic Reconnaissance Unit and No 421 Flight.

Aircraft of the Photographic Reconnaissance Unit and No 421 Flight were to be coloured and marked in accordance with their operational requirements, and their colour schemes did not always conform to the norm for each aircraft type. Special arrangements had to be made by these units with HQ Fighter Command to try and ensure the safety of aircraft so coloured and marked.

Section II was entitled 'Markings on British Aircraft, including American and Allied Types in use by British Air Forces'. The National markings to be carried were as follows.
Upper surfaces
Red and blue roundels were to be carried on the uppersurfaces of the wing tips.
Sides of fuselage
A red, white, and blue roundel surrounded by a yellow ring was to be carried on each side of the fuselage.
Fin markings
Vertical red, white and blue stripes (with red leading) each of 8 inch widths and 27 inches in height were to be applied to the

side of the fin against the rudder hinge post immediately above the tail plane. The resulting marking was to form a rectangle 24 inches wide by 27 inches high or an area as closely conforming to this as the size and shape of the fin permitted.
Under surfaces
Roundels were not to be carried on the undersurfaces of operational aircraft, except for Day Fighters which were to carry red, white, and blue roundels. The roundel on the black undersurfaces of the port wing of Day Fighters was to be surrounded by a yellow ring.

Registration Number (serial number). The registration number allotted to the aircraft was to be carried by all aircraft at the rear of the fuselage. Training aircraft in the Flying Training Command and Technical Training Command also carried their registration numbers on the under surfaces of the wing.

Special Markings
Day Fighters were to carry an 18 inch wide band of duck egg blue (Sky Type S) right around the fuselage immediately forward of the tailplane, and were to have the airscrew spinner painted duck egg blue (Sky Type S).

Non operational aircraft with yellow undersurfaces were allowed to carry large figures on the sides of the fuselage so that they might meet training requirements. Ambulance aircraft which carried the 'Geneva' Red Cross on a white disc of the same diameter as the yellow ring of the standard roundel were allowed to carry the special marking immediately aft of the roundel on each side of the fuselage.

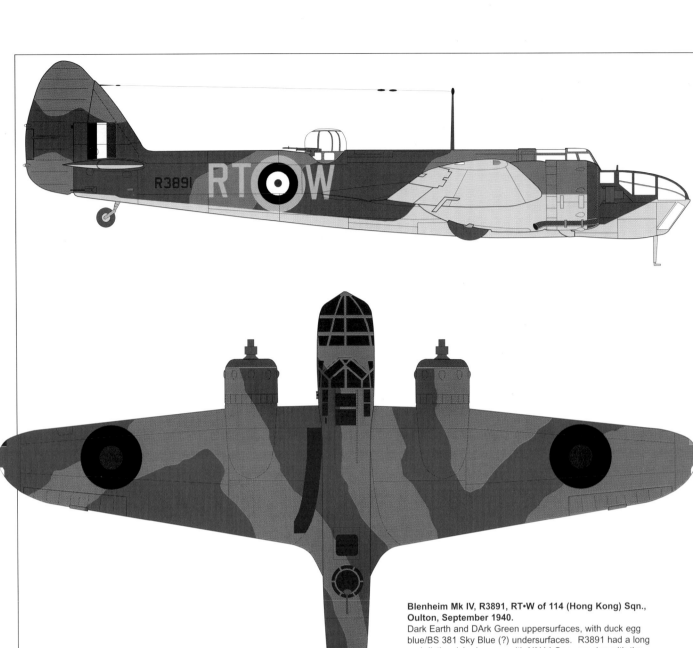

Blenheim Mk IV, R3891, RT•W of 114 (Hong Kong) Sqn., Oulton, September 1940.
Dark Earth and DArk Green uppersurfaces, with duck egg blue/BS 381 Sky Blue (?) undersurfaces. R3891 had a long and distinguished career with N°114 Sqn., serving with the unit from early 1940 in France, until late 1941, and is illustrated here in the scheme described by its regular pilot for much of that time, (then) Sgt Terry Staples.

Night / black

Dark Earth   Dark Green

Duck Egg Blue   Medium Sea Grey

Red   White

Blue   Yellow

Examples of Allied Air Force markings

Poland   Czechoslovakia   Netherlands

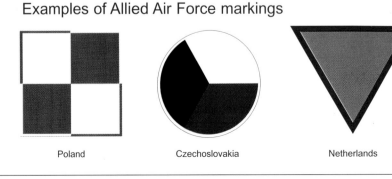

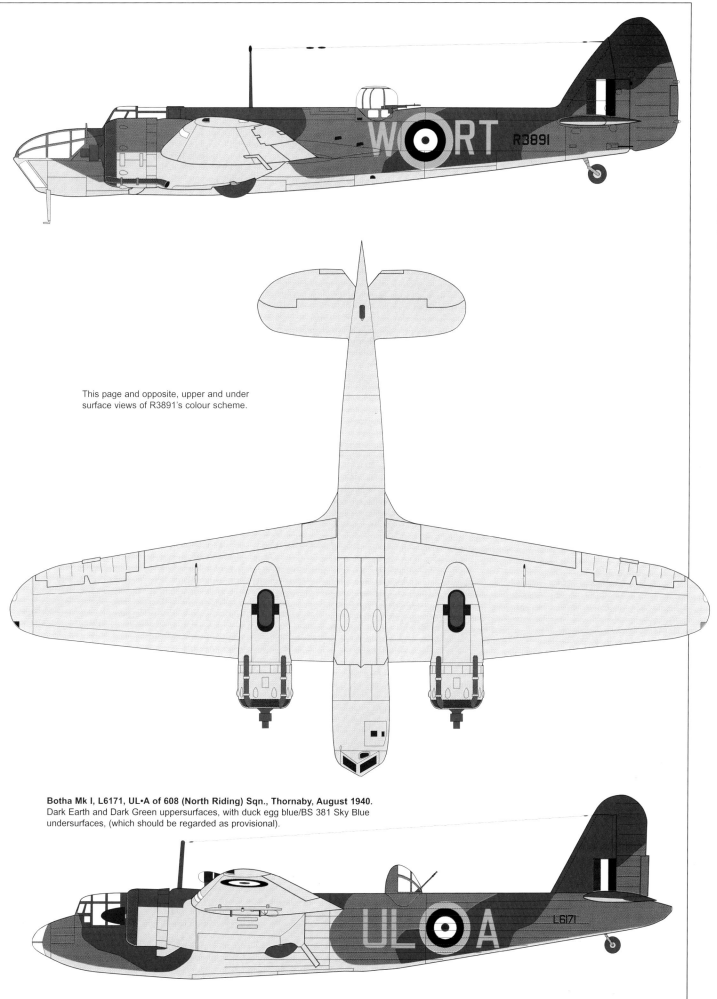

This page and opposite, upper and under surface views of R3891's colour scheme.

Botha Mk I, L6171, UL•A of 608 (North Riding) Sqn., Thornaby, August 1940.
Dark Earth and Dark Green uppersurfaces, with duck egg blue/BS 381 Sky Blue undersurfaces, (which should be regarded as provisional).

CHAPTER 10
MATERIALS - 1939 to 1940

Aircraft Design Memorandum 332, Issue 2, dated 8 September 1939, listed five material specifications for top coat camouflage finishes on RAF aircraft. These were Air Ministry Directorate of Technical Development Material Specification DTD 308 Matt Cellulose Finishes and Primer, issued in July 1936; DTD 314 Matt Pigmented Oil Varnishes and Primer, issued in September 1936; DTD 83A Aeroplane Doping Schemes of December 1935; DTD 63A Cellulose Enamels and Primer (For Metals and Timber), issued in April 1939; and DTD 260A Pigmented Oil Varnishes and Primer (For Metals and Timber) date of issue unknown but reprinted in August 1940.

DTD 308 was the Material Specification for a cellulose based material consisting of a pigmented primer suitable for direct application to metal or timber, and a pigmented cellulose finishing coating suitable for application over the primer - suitable for application by brush or spray. The finishing coating was available in two types, one of which was suitable for use under normal (temperate climate) atmospheric conditions, and the other which was suitable for use under adverse (tropical climate) conditions. The resulting dry film from such an application should match the standard which was obtainable from the Director of Aeronautical Inspection in mattness, colour, and smoothness of finish.

DTD 314 was the Material

Specification for a synthetic finishing material which specified that the materials would consist of a pigmented primer suitable for direct application to metal or timber and a pigmented oil varnish suitable for applicaton over the primer by means of brush or spray.

DTD 83A was the Material Specification for the cellulose based material used to first prime, (when the red oxide of iron pigment specified for this purpose bestowed the familiar dull red colour), and then finish those airframe components covered with linen fabric to BS Specification F.1 in its latest issue. It specified that any aeroplane doping scheme employed would comply with BS Specification D.101 Properties of Aeroplane Doping Scheme in its latest issue and that the said doping schemes would consist of pigmented solutions of nitro-cellulose, pigmented solutions of cellulose acetate for the first coats and of pigmented solutions of nitro-cellulose for the finishing coats, or any such other materials as might be approved from time to time.

DTD 63A was the Material Specification for Cellulose Enamels and Primer which could be used on Metals or Timber. The materials were to consist of a pigmented primer suitable for direct application to metal or timber; and a pigmented cellulose enamel which was to

be suitable for application over the primer. The pigmented cellulose enamel was to dry to a uniformly smooth covering which had a glossy finish.

In March 1940, as this Material Specification was being applied to Blenheim bombers on the production line, the Specification was amended in that the requirement that the finishing coat should dry having a glossy finish was deleted. Thereafter it seems to have been referred to as 'DTD 63 with reduced gloss'.

DTD 260A was the Material Specification for Pigmented Oil Varnishes and Primer for Metals and Timber. The materials were to consist of a pigmented primer suitable for direct application to metal or timber; and a pigmented oil varnish suitable for application over the primer. When dry, it should have a glossy finish. The colour of the material was to be one of the British Standard colours listed in the latest issue of BS Specification No 381, or when an Aluminium finish was required, the Standard was obtainable from the Director of Aeronautical Inspection at the Air Ministry, and later the Ministry of Aircraft Production.

During the course of 1940, these Specifications were joined by two new Specifications, DTD 420 Material Specification for Matt Pigmented Lanolin

Heading: Blenheim If, L8679, BQ•O of 600 Sqn. Delivered to the RAF before the outbreak of war, this aircraft would have been finished in the original matt finish paint to either DTD 308 or DTD 314 on its metal parts and Dope to DTD 83A on its fabric parts. Note the serial number repeated on the rudder, a left-over from pre-war days, and the Night/White undersurfaces possibly dating this aircraft to prior early June 1940.

Right: Lysander Mk II, N1256, LX•M of 225 Sqn., whose largely fabric covered airframe would have been finished throughout in materials to DTD 83A. Note the light coloured mainwheel hubs.

and Resin Finishes, issued in March 1940; and DTD 441 Material Specification for Matt Finish Distemper, issued in August 1940.

DTD 420 was the Material Specification for Matt Pigmented Lanolin and Resin Finishes, first issued in March 1940. The material was a pigmented solution of lanolin and resin in white spirit which was at first only available in the colours of the Temperate Sea Scheme - ie Light Slate Grey, Dark Slate Grey, Dark Sea Grey, and Extra Dark Sea Grey. In September 1940, Amendment List No 1 added Sky to this list of colours.

DTD 441 was the Material Specification for Matt Finish Distemper, issued in August 1940. The material was to consist of a smooth distemper suitable for application to doped fabric or painted metal surfaces by brush or spray, or it could be supplied in the form of a paste or powder which, when mixed with water in amounts to be stated by the supplier, would produce a distemper.

One coat of the material when applied to a fabric or metal surface covered with Identification Yellow was to match the standard in colour, finish and opacity. After drying at room temperature for two weeks, the material was to be readily removable with hot water leaving the painted or doped surfaces uninjured. The colour standards were available from the Director of Aeronautical Inspection at the MAP. The material specification for gas detector paint is unknown.

To enable the type of finishing material used on a component to be identified should it become necessary to repair it, the DTD specification number was to be stencilled on each component. The letter 'C' indicated a cellulose finish and the letter 'S' indicated a synthetic finish. The letter 'C' or 'S' was to be stencilled immediately below the specification number, and the whole

Spitfire Mk I, X4593, UO·A of 266 Sqn., photographed at Wittering in July/August, and finished in the correct paint specifications for camouflage colours and identification markings of the mid/late-1940 Battle of Britain period. Note the full height, 8 inch wide fin stripes and the oversize 7 inch red centre to the fuselage roundel - a peculiarity seen on many Spitfires of the mid-late 1940/early 1941 period.

marking was to be executed in letters 1 inch high in Red on black or Night surfaces, and in Night on all other colours. For example:

DTD 308
C

Where the letter 'S' was applied in such a marking it should not be confused with the 'Type S' suffix which began to be applied to the new smooth paints which began to be introduced during 1940 which could be either cellulose or synthetic based.

Occasionally, a dope manufacturer's own specification such as Cellon X might be used. The colour photographs 13 and 14 on the inside back cover show the method and style in which this was marked onto the rudder, in this case of an unidentified Spitfire. The letters 'CX' are just under 1 inch high, and just over three quarters of an inch wide, applied in Night.

During 1940, the following DTD material specifications were issued:-
DTD 420 for Matt Pigmented Lanolin & Resin Finishes and an amended version of DTD 63A were issued in March; DTD 441 for Matt Finish Distemper in August; and DTD 911 which was a process specification rather than a purely material specification for the Protection of Magnesium Rich Alloy Parts Against Corrosion in November.

Stores Reference Numbers for paint materials from the RAF Vocabulary of Stores are listed here. Typically, three Stores Reference Numbers are given for each colour to each material specification. These signify half gallon, one gallon, and five gallon size containers in that order of Reference Number. Unfortunately the author does not have a complete listing for the 1940 period, and the listing given here has many gaps, some of them quite large. The usual practice when new listings were issued was for the old one to be removed and destroyed. As a consequence, very little documentation of this kind appears to have survived from 1940. The colours are listed here in numerical order as this helps convey the order in which they became available. There is just one reference to DTD 63, and none at all for gas detector paint.

Vocabulary of Stores reference 33B/

157 Grey
158 Aluminium 1 Gal DTD 260.
161 Gloss White DTD 260.
164/165 Blue DTD308
166/167 Red DTD 308
168/169 White DTD 308
170/171 Yellow DTD 308
172/173 Blue DTD 314
174/175 Red DTD 314
176/177 White DTD 314
178/179 Yellow DTD 314
180-182 Dark Earth DTD 83A
183-185 Dark Green DTD 83A
186-188 Night DTD 83A
189-191 Dark Earth DTD 308
192-194 Dark Green DTD 308
195-197 Night DTD 308
198-200 Dark Earth DTD 314
201-203 Dark Green DTD 314
204-206 Night DTD 314
207-209 Dark Grey Primer DTD 308
210-212 Dark Grey Primer DTD 314
213 Yellow Primer.
218-221 Dark Sea Grey DTD 83A
222-224 Dark Slate Grey DTD 83A
225-227 Extra Dark Sea Grey DTD 83A
228-230 Light Earth DTD 83A
231-233 Light Green DTD 83A
234-236 Light Slate Grey DTD 83A
237-239 Dark Sea Grey DTD 308
240-242 Dark Slate Grey DTD308 :
243-245 Extra Dark Sea Grey DTD 308
246-248 Light Earth DTD308
249-251 Light Green DTD 308
252-254 Light Slate Grey DTD 308
260-262 Light Grey Primer DTD308
263-265 Sky Grey DTD 308
266-268 Sky Blue DTD 308
269-271 Light Green DTD 314
272-274 Light Earth DTD 314
275-277 Dark Slate Grey DTD 314
278-280 Light Slate Grey DTD 314
281-283 Extra Dark Sea Grey DTD 314
284-286 Dark Sea Grey DTD 314
287-289 Sky Grey DTD 314
290-292 Sky Blue DTD 314
293-295 Sky Grey DTD 83A
296-298 Sky Blue DTD 83A
299 Special Night DTD RDM2
317 Aluminium DTD 63 1 Gal
318 Dark Mediterranean Blue Cellulose 5 Gal
319 Light Mediterranean Blue Cellulose 5 Gal
330-332 Sky DTD 308
333-335 Sky DTD 83A
336-338 Sky DTD 314
340 Thinner for DTD RDM2A
341 Blue Synthetic 5 Gal
342 Red Synthetic 5 Gal
343 White DTD 314 5 Gal
344 Yellow DTD 314 5 Gal
345 Sea Grey Medium DTD 314 5 Gal
347 Light Mediterranean Blue Synthetic 5 Gal
354 Light Mediterranean Blue Synthetic 1 Gal
355 Light Mediterranean Blue Synthetic 1 Gal
356 Midstone Cellulose 5 Gal
357 Dark Earth DTD 441
358 Dark Green DTD 441
359 Special Night DTD 441
367 Aluminium DTD 420
368 Dark Sea Grey DTD 420
369 Dark Slate Grey DTD 420
370 Extra Dark Sea Grey DTD 420
371 Light Slate Grey DTD 420
372 Sky DTD 420
375 Special Night DTD RDM2A
376 White
378 Azure Blue Cellulose 5 gal Overseas

Azure Blue was named at the RAE, on or about, 4 December, and so marks the approximate limit of the allocation of stores reference numbers up to the end of 1940.

CHAPTER 11
EXCEPTIONS TO THE RULE

September 1939 - December 1940

It is often said that there is always an exception to every rule, but in the case of RAF camouflage and markings during 1940 there were two. The first exception was noted by DTD Technical Circular No 83 in August 1940, and what had by that time become the Photographic Reconnaissance Unit.

The origins of this unit have already been briefly dealt with in a previous chapter where the origins of Sky were examined. To recap, this unit had been set up as a result of a meeting held at the Air Ministry on 22 March 1939, where it was decided to form an experimental unit for the purpose of testing, and if successful, developing, what were then considered novel techniques for making photo reconnaissance sorties over enemy territory. The basis of the scheme proposed was the use of high speed and invisibility, and the originator of the scheme, F S Cotton was put in charge. At this time the unit seems to have been a civilian one working under contract to the Air Ministry, but this arrangement seems to have come to an end with the outbreak of war with the unit being absorbed into the RAF on or about 22 September. Cotton was given the substantive rank of Squadron Leader, (acting Wing Commander), and placed in command.

Mention has already been made of the units initial equipment of Blenheims being too slow and of the work undertaken to 'streamline' them, including the use of the duck egg green colour called Camotint, later named Sky by the RAE, to make them less visible from below.

Early in October the unit came under the control of Fighter Command and fierce lobbying of the unit's new masters eventually saw a Spitfire delivered which was modified for the PR role. Finished in all over duck egg green Camotint, this aircraft was despatched to France in early November supported by a Hudson and a Lockheed 12A, where they were collectively known as the Special Survey Flight. A number of experimental operational flights were carried out which conclusively proved that the concept worked, and at the end of November 1939, the chief of the Air Staff decided that the unit should be expanded.

This led to the acquisition of more Spitfires and the introduction of a new camouflage colour. Once again, the material was supplied by Titanine and was quite glossy. It apparently went by the name of Cosmic in the Titanine catalogue and was a darkish blue grey with a hint of green about it. Whilst described variously as Cosmic, or electric blue, when this colour was accepted into the Vocabulary of Stores in 1941 it became simply known as PRU Blue after the unit which had first used it and continued to be its main user. Eyewitness accounts indicate that this colour first

began to appear on Spitfires in February 1940.

There was however an element of risk in using unfamiliar colour schemes, especially when they were applied to a less familiar type. Evidence of this is provided by the loss of Hudson N7334 on 3 March 1940. This aircraft was tasked with photographing several airfields in Southern England for the benefit of the French Air Force. On arrival in the vicinity of Gravesend however, the Hudson was intercepted and shot down by friendly fighters.

Some mention was apparently made of the Hudson's colour scheme being a factor in the misidentification of the aircraft at the Court of Enquiry which was subsequently held, as a series of photographs of a similarly camouflaged Hudson were taken for the Courts' benefit. These photographs show the pattern, although not the colours of the scheme which is illustrated here.

Apparently as a consequence of this loss two steps were taken to try to prevent it happening again. Firstly, on or about 13 March 1940, the Operational Commands appear to have been notified that aircraft of non standard colouring might occasionally be seen in the east and south east of Great Britain, and that such aircraft belonged to the PDU. The basic colouring was said to be a greenish blue, and some aircraft were camouflaged on the top surfaces while others were not. All had roundels, but

Heading: PRU Spitfire, R6903, converted into a PR 1C in August 1940, (with one of this specialised unit's Hudsons in the background), probably painted in the darkish blue-grey shade, originally called Cosmic, which evolved into the colour PRU Blue, named after the unit. Note the LY code letters, allocated in June/July 1940, the small serial number, fuselage roundel with very narrow yellow outer ring and small fin flash.

Right: Another of the PRU's special Spitfires, N3117, which was modified several times during its service, and looks to have been painted in Sky. Note the small numeral 3 under the serial number.

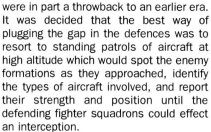

they were not conspicuous. The types which were painted in this way were listed as Hudson, Blenheim, Spitfire, Harvard, Lockheed 18A Beechcraft, and Lockheed Spartan, and it was noted that other types might be painted in the future. It was pointed out that as the colour scheme was somewhat similar to that adopted by the *Luftwaffe*, (presumably a reference to the Hudson's scheme), all pilots were to be acquainted with these facts.

Secondly, in early April 1940, the PDU circulated three colour paintings showing the colour schemes then in use on its aircraft. The first two consisted of a Spitfire and Blenheim in overall Sky with red, white and blue roundels in all six positions. The third diagram showed the Hudson in this scheme. Unfortunately, the colours used on the paintings appear to be representative only, and whilst Sky is easy to determine on all three, the shade of green and grey or grey/green on the upper surfaces of the Hudson are not. No document seen by the author positively identifies them either.

Sometime in May, June, or early July, the PDU was allocated the letters 'LY' to serve as the two letter unit identification marking. Prior to this no such markings had been carried, with the aircraft only being marked by its serial number, (which was sometimes painted out), and a small number applied underneath it, presumably to serve as some kind of individual identification marking within the unit. The 'LY' code letters were shown in a further batch of three colour paintings issued to the Operational Commands following the unit's transfer to the operational control of Coastal Command on 18 June 1940.

The drawings, issued on 21 July 1940, showed two Spitfires, one of which was a pale green, and the other of which was a blue; both of which shared identical markings. These consisted of red, white, and blue roundels on top of, and underneath, the mainplane; red, white, and blue roundels surrounded by a narrow yellow ring on the fuselage; and small red, white, and blue fin stripes.

The third diagram showed a Hudson, but in place of the earlier non standard disruptive pattern of three colours on the upper surfaces, there was now something more like a standard two colour pattern, executed in grey and green. The undersurfaces remained Sky. National markings consisted of red and blue roundels on the wing uppersurfaces with red, white, and blue roundels below,

whilst the fuselage also carried red, white, and blue roundels, but this time surrounded by a narrow yellow ring. The fin was marked with red, white and blue stripes which were carried up the full height of the fin. All three aircraft carried the 'LY' codes in light grey aft of the fuselage roundel. Aircraft finished in these schemes were said to be operating from Heston, Wick, and St Eval.

Once again the colours used in these colour paintings were nothing more than representative, bearing little resemblance to the colours which were probably used.

Fighter Command tried to describe these colours in layman's terms in a letter to all its Groups, Anti-Aircraft Command, and Coastal Command on 25 July. Spitfires were said to be painted all over either in "electric blue" which is thought to be a reference to Cosmic; or "a pale greenish buff" which is almost certainly a reference to Sky. The Hudson was described as being camouflaged on the upper surfaces in "olive green" and "dark grey". In the light of subsequent events within Coastal Command, it would appear that the colours used on the uppersurfaces of the Hudson at this time were those of the Temperate Sea Scheme - Extra Dark Sea Grey and Dark Slate Grey. The undersurfaces were described as "a pale greenish buff". It is interesting to note that by this date, the Air Ministry term 'duck egg blue' does not yet seem to have caught on!

As mentioned previously, the conference held on 23 July agreed to allow the unit to continue to use its non standard colour schemes as long as the Air Ministry was kept informed of their nature, and this fact was circulated in DTD Technical Circular No 83 on 23 August 1940. This writ then appears to have run for the rest of the year, also being included in AMO A.926 which was published on 12 December 1940.

421 Flight

The second exception was made for the aircraft of 421 Flight. When the Germans switched their tactics to high altitude raids by a mixed force of pure fighters and fighter-bombers during October, the RAF found that for a variety of technical reasons, such raids were difficult to spot and track. Even when this was possible, the comparatively high speed and altitude at which these aircraft operated made the raids difficult to intercept.

As a consequence, Fighter Command was forced to resort to new tactics which

were in part a throwback to an earlier era. It was decided that the best way of plugging the gap in the defences was to resort to standing patrols of aircraft at high altitude which would spot the enemy formations as they approached, identify the types of aircraft involved, and report their strength and position until the defending fighter squadrons could effect an interception.

To undertake this task, a new unit, 421 (Reconnaissance) Flight, was formed on 8 October at Gravesend from a nucleus of 66 Squadron, and was initially equipped with some of the first Hurricane Mk IIs. The pilots were tasked with flying individual sorties throughout the daylight hours in order to spot any incoming raids. Because their task was to observe and report back, pilots were instructed to avoid engaging the enemy unless they were obliged to do so, an instruction which was at least in part encouraged by the fact that in order to improve the high altitude performance of the aircraft, they were flown with only two of the machine guns loaded. Despite the improved performance of the new Hurricane Mk II, they did not prove popular with the pilots who complained to Fighter Command. As a result the unit re equipped with Spitfire Mk IIs at the end of October, which proved to be much more popular and better suited to the work.

At first the patrols were made by single aircraft, but eventually it was decided that it would be prudent to mount patrols of two aircraft so that each could watch the others tail. 421 Flight successfully carried out its operational role for the rest of the year eventually settling at Hawkinge from mid-November onwards after spending a short time first at West Malling and then Biggin Hill. 421 Flight was brought up to squadron strength and re-numbered as 91 Squadron on 11 January 1941.

Presumably as a result of the close ties between 421 Flight and its 'parent' unit 66 Squadron, 421 Flight used the same two letter code combination, LZ, but separated them by the addition of a hyphen or dash, usually applied as a small square thus, L-Z. Like aircraft of the Photographic Reconnaissance Unit, aircraft of 421 Flight were allowed to be coloured and marked in accordance with their operational requirements and their colour schemes did not always conform to the norm for each aircraft type. Special arrangements had to be made by these units with HQ Fighter Command to try and ensure the safety of aircraft so coloured and marked.

Unfortunately, exact details of this unit's camouflage and markings are largely unknown. However, Spitfire Mk II, P7498 L-Z•K is thought to have been coloured overall blue. Unfortunately it is not known which shade!

Spitfire Mk II, P7531, L-Z•I of 421 (Reconnaissance) Flight circa November 1940. This particular aircraft is in standard Fighter Command colours, although at least one Spitfire, P7498, is thought to have been painted 'Sky Blue' overall!

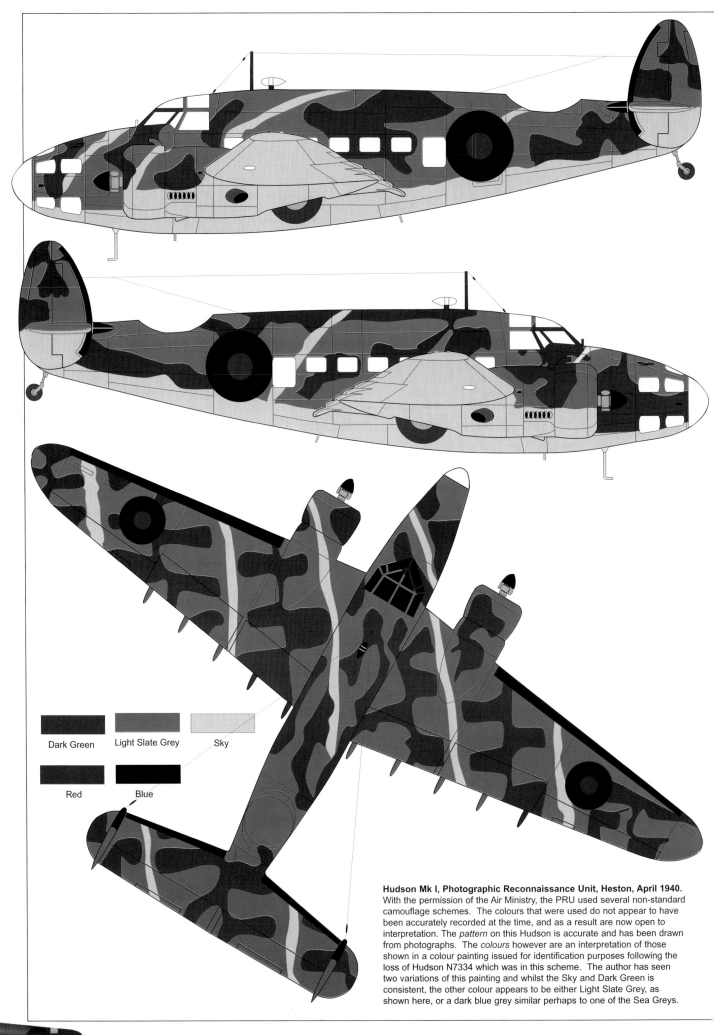

Dark Green | Light Slate Grey | Sky

Red | Blue

Hudson Mk I, Photographic Reconnaissance Unit, Heston, April 1940.
With the permission of the Air Ministry, the PRU used several non-standard camouflage schemes. The colours that were used do not appear to have been accurately recorded at the time, and as a result are now open to interpretation. The *pattern* on this Hudson is accurate and has been drawn from photographs. The *colours* however are an interpretation of those shown in a colour painting issued for identification purposes following the loss of Hudson N7334 which was in this scheme. The author has seen two variations of this painting and whilst the Sky and Dark Green is consistent, the other colour appears to be either Light Slate Grey, as shown here, or a dark blue grey similar perhaps to one of the Sea Greys.

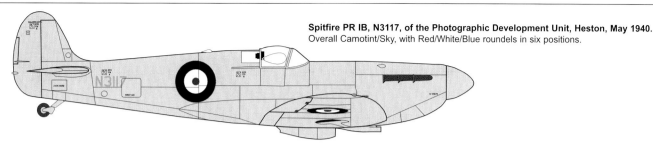

Spitfire PR IB, N3117, of the Photographic Development Unit, Heston, May 1940.
Overall Camotint/Sky, with Red/White/Blue roundels in six positions.

Spitfire PR IE, N3117 of the PRU, Heston, July 1940.
The same aircraft as that illustrated above, but modified into PR IE standard. The author is convinced that the scheme remained overall Camotint/Sky, but the artist is equally adamant that the pilot claimed it was a very pale shade of pink - (possibly repainted in this colour in 1941?) - so both schemes have been illustrated! Note the Medium Sea Grey code letters, smaller serial number presentation and small numeral 3 beneath the serial number.

Dark Earth	Dark Green
Sky	PRU Blue
Night / black	Medium Sea Grey
Red	White
Blue	Yellow

PRU Pink

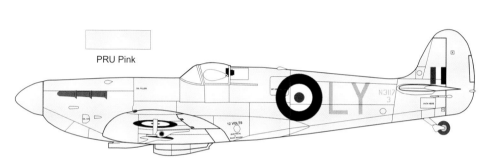

Spitfire PR IC, P9385, of the PRU, Heston, September 1940.
Overall Cosmic/PRU Blue, with Red/White/Blue roundels in six positions, those on the fuselage sides very thinly outlined in Yellow. Cosmic which was later named PRU Blue, was included in the post-war Ministry of Supply colour range as Aircraft Finish N°14, and was included in BS 381C 1964 as N°636 PRU Blue. The closest FS 595B colour is 35189.

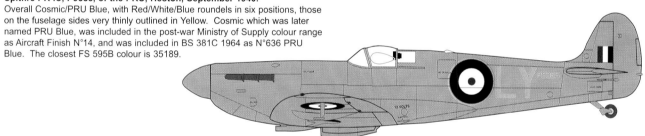

Spitfire Mk II, P7531, L-Z•I of 421 (Reconnaissance) Flight, Gravesend, November 1940.
Dark Earth and Dark Green uppersurfaces with Sky undersurfaces. Note that 421 Flight's codes were separated by a hyphen. Underwing roundels may have been applied by this time.

Spitfire Mk II, P7498, L-Z•K of 421 (Reconnaissance) Flight, Gravesend, October/November 1940.
A very provisional illustration of how P7498 *might* have looked in overall BS 381 (1930) Sky Blue.

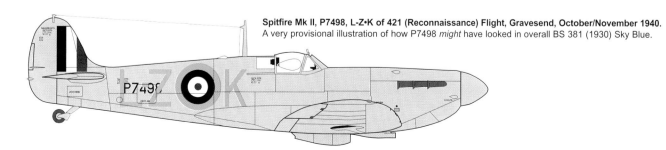

CHAPTER 12
COLOURS

Colour Standards

During the development phase of aircraft camouflage before the war, standards for the various camouflage and identification colours were produced in small numbers by the RAE. These apparently took the form of brushed out samples of dope on small pieces of fabric and brushed out samples of paint on small pieces of aluminium.

The first attempt to reproduce colour standards for widespread use by the Aeronautical Inspection Directorate took the form of printed colour cards which were stuck inside a small booklet. These were manufactured for the Air Ministry by the Mitchell Colour Card Company and were delivered in February 1939.

The 18 camouflage colours contained in this first issue of colour standards were as follows: Dark Earth, Light Earth, Dark Green, Light Green, Extra Dark Sea Green, Dark Sea Green, Light Sea Green, Dark Mediterranean Blue, Light Mediterranean Blue, Extra Dark Sea Grey, Dark Sea Grey, Dark Sand, Dark Red Sand, Red Sand, Light Sand, Dark Slate Grey, Light Slate Grey, and Night.

Of these colours Extra Dark Sea Green, Dark Sea Green, Light Sea Green,

Dark Sand, Dark Red Sand, Red Sand, Light Sand, Dark Mediterranean Blue and Light Mediterranean Blue were fro Tropical schemes intended for overseas and are therefore outside the scope of this particular book.

Whilst it is possible that the Mediterranean Blues could have been used as undersurface colours in the UK during this period, there appears to be no evidence that this happened.

Colours which were added to the Air Ministry's list of camouflage colours after this standard was published, are Sky Blue and Special Night in 1939, followed by Sky, Middle Stone, and Azure Blue during 1940. Because Azure Blue was not 'invented' and named until December 1940, its use as an undersurface colour during the daylight battles of the summer is highly unlikely. It has therefore been omitted.

When the Ministry of Aircraft Production was formed in 1940, it took over the responsibility for producing colour standards for aircraft paints from the Air Ministry. The MAP Standards took the form of samples of paint applied to cards which were bound into small booklets. When the MAP was absorbed

into the Ministry of Supply on 1 April 1946, the MoS took over the responsibility for aircraft colour standards. These appear to have taken the form of painted sheets of card, each enclosed in an envelope which were then bound in a ring binder and entitled 'Ministry of Supply Standard of Colour Gloss and Smoothness for Aircraft Finishes Supplementary to BSS 381'.

The fact that the MoS Standards were supplementary to BSS 381 is quite important as it was not until 1964 that aircraft colours were included in BS 381C. Such aircraft colours which were in various editions of BS 381 prior to 1964 were there because they were colours which were already in BSS 381, (which was first issued in 1930), when they were chosen for an aircraft application. This means that it is inaccurate to refer to most British military aircraft colours prior to 1964 by using its BS 381 number and name. Anyone intending to obtain a copy of BS 381C, (as it became in 1948), should note that they will require the 1930 and 1964 editions, now long out of print, as subsequent editions dropped several of the aircraft colours mentioned here.

Heading: Spitfire Mk I, X4474, QV·I of 19 Sqn., (also illustrated on the front cover), epitomising the RAF Day Fighter scheme of 1940. Uppersurfaces were Dark Earth and Dark Green, with what was euphemistically termed Sky, (duck egg blue or duck egg green), on the undersurfaces. Whilst there is no dispute about the uppersurface colours, it is virtually impossible to tell from black and white photographs such as those in this book, what colour the undersurfaces *actually* were.

Right: Wellington Ic, T2468, WS·Y of 9 Sqn., shows the late 1940 camouflage scheme for Night Bombers. Uppersurfaces were Dark Green and Dark Earth, with Special Night undersurfaces. Squadron codes and serial numbers at this time were Medium Sea Grey.

Camouflage Colours

Dark Green

Introduced in 1936, Dark Green was used as part of the disruptive camouflage pattern with Dark Earth in the Temperate Land Scheme. It continued to be used throughout the rest of the war and was included in the post war MoS colour range as Aircraft Finish No 7. In 1964 Aircraft Finish No 7 was included in BS 381C as No 641 Dark Green. This number was something of an error which does not appear to have been corrected until the 1988 edition when the number was changed to No 241.
Colour matched by BS381C No 241 Dark Green and FS 595B 34079

Dark Earth

Introduced in 1936, Dark Earth was used as part of the disruptive camouflage pattern with Dark Green in the Temperate Land Scheme. It continued to be used throughout the rest of the war and was included in the post-war MoS colour range as Aircraft Finish No 13. In 1964 Aircraft Finish No 13 was included in BS 381C as No 450 Dark Earth. Colour matched by BS 381C No 450 Dark Earth. The closest FS 595B match is 30118

Light Green

Introduced in 1939, Light Green was used with Light Earth as a 'compensating shadow shade' in the Temperate Land Scheme applied to biplanes. Light Green was applied to the lower wing and sides of the fuselage where its lighter tone would help offset the shadow thrown by the upper wing and side of the fuselage itself, in an attempt to make the aircraft appear to be one even tone and thus avoid an eye catching contrast. Light Green fell from use post-war and was not included in the MoS colour range.
The closest FS 595B match is 34102

Light Earth

Introduced in 1939, Light Earth was used with Light Green as a 'compensating shadow shade' in the Temperate Land Scheme as applied to biplanes. Light Earth was applied to the lower wing and sides of the fuselage where its lighter tone would help offset the shadow thrown by the upper wing and side of the fuselage itself, in an attempt to make the aircraft appear to be one even tone and thus avoid an eye catching contrast. Light Earth fell from use post-war and was not included in the MoS colour range.
The closest FS 595B match is 30257

Dark Slate Grey

Introduced in 1939 Dark Slate Grey was used with Extra Dark Sea Grey in the Temperate Sea Scheme. It was used throughout the rest of the war but fell from use thereafter and was not included the the MoS colour range.
There is no close match for this colour in FS 595B. The green/grey hue of this colour lies about half way between 34096 and 36118.

Light Slate Grey

Introduced in 1939, Light Slate Grey was used with Dark Sea Grey as a 'compensating shadow shade' in the Temperate Sea Scheme. Light Slate Grey was applied to the lower wing and sides of the fuselage where its lighter tone would help offset the shadow thrown by the upper wing and side of the fuselage itself, in an attempt to make the aircraft appear to be one even tone and thus avoid an eye catching contrast. Light Slate Grey continued to be used as a markings colour by the RAF post-war and was included in the MoS colour range as Aircraft Finish No 3. In 1964 Aircraft Finish No 3 was included in BS 381C as No 639 Light Slate Grey.
Colour matched by BS 381C No 639 Light Slate Grey. The closest FS 595B match is 34159.

Extra Dark Sea Grey

Introduced in 1939, Extra Dark Sea Grey was used with Dark Slate Grey in the Temperate Sea Scheme. It was used throughout the rest of the war and its continuing use by Naval Aviation post-war saw its inclusion in the MoS colour range as Aircraft Finish No 6.
In 1964 Aircraft Finish No6 was included in BS 381C as No 640 Extra Dark Sea Grey.
Colour matched by BS 381C as No 640 Extra Dark Sea Grey. The closest FS 595B match is 36099.

Dark Sea Grey

Introduced in 1939, Dark Sea Grey was used with Light Slate Grey as a 'compensating shadow shade' in the Temperate Sea Scheme. Dark Sea Grey was applied to the lower wing and sides of the fuselage where its lighter tone would help offset the shadow thrown by the upper wing and side of the fuselage itself, in an attempt to make the aircraft appear to be one even tone and thus avoid an eye catching contrast. Dark Sea Grey continued to be used by the RAF post-war and was included in the MoS colour range as Aircraft Finish No 5. In 1964 Aircraft Finish No 5 was included in BS 381C as No 638 Dark Sea Grey.
Colour matched by BS 381C No 638 Dark Sea Grey. The closest FS 595B match is 36118.

Sky Grey

Introduced in 1939, Sky Grey was intended for use on the undersurfaces of Fleet Air Arm aircraft. Archealogical evidence shows that it was used on the undersurfaces of several different types of day flying aircraft during 1940. It fell from use post-war and was not included in the MoS colour range.
The closest FS 595B match is 36463

Sky Blue

Introduced from 1939, Sky Blue was originally intended for use on radio controlled de Havilland Queen Wasp target aircraft. During December 1940, it was apparently used to apply the tail band and spinner recognition markings to Day Fighters. It fell from use post-war and was not included in the MoS colour range.
The closest FS 595B match is 35550

BSS 381 (1930) No1 Sky Blue

(Known colloquially as 'Duck Egg Blue'?) Apparently used on the undersurfaces of day flying aircraft during 1940, Sky Blue was included in the 1930 edition of BSS 381 and was therefore probably available to aircraft material specifications DTD 63A and DTD 260A during 1940. Its aquamarine hue may be the origin of the term 'Duck Egg Blue' which is a good colloquial description of this colour. Archaeological evidence indicates that this colour had a gloss finish which ties in with the requirements of DTD 63A and DTD 260A.
The closest FS 595B match is 14325

BSS 381 (1930) No 16 Eau de Nil

(Known colloquially as 'Duck Egg Green'?) Apparently used on the undersurfaces of day flying aircraft during 1940, Eau de Nil was included in the 1930 edition of BSS 381 and was therefore probably available to aircraft material specifications DTD 63A and DTD 260A during 1940. Its grey/green hue may be described as 'a rich Duck Egg Green' which is a good colloquial description of this colour. Archaeological evidence indicates that this colour had a gloss finish which ties in with the requirements of DTD 63A and DTD 260A
The closest FS 595B match is 14533

'Light Blue-Grey'

The origin and true identity of this colour has not been properly identified at the time of writing. There is a possibility that this was the shade of grey, 33B/157, which was originally specified for the application of code letters in 1939. Several eyewitnesses have described the colour of the pre-war code letters as being 'light blue', perhaps as an optical illusion brought about by using a grey colour which had a very strong blue element to it on a Dark Earth/Dark Green background. A colour answering to this description was possibly applied to Blenheims just prior to their despatch to France in 1939. The colour referred to here as 'Light Blue-Grey' was found on the underside of Hurricane Mk I, P2728, which was lost on 9 September 1940.
The closest FS 595B match is 35414 but this is too dark and too green

Night

This colour was first introduced in 1937 and was not a true 'black', being instead a very dark blue-grey made up from a mix of carbon black and ultramarine blue pigments. It was included in the MoS colour range as Aircraft Finish No 8 and included in BS 381C as No 642 in 1964. It is interesting to note that Night was still being listed in the Vocab of Stores as a separate colour from Black in the mid-1960s.
Colour matched by BS 381C No 642 Night and FS 595B 37030

Special Night RDM2 and RDM2A

This colour was introduced in September 1939, and unlike Night was a true 'sooty' black. Used as the undersurface finish for night bombers, it remained in use for this purpose until December 1942 when it was abandoned in favour of Night, the colour it

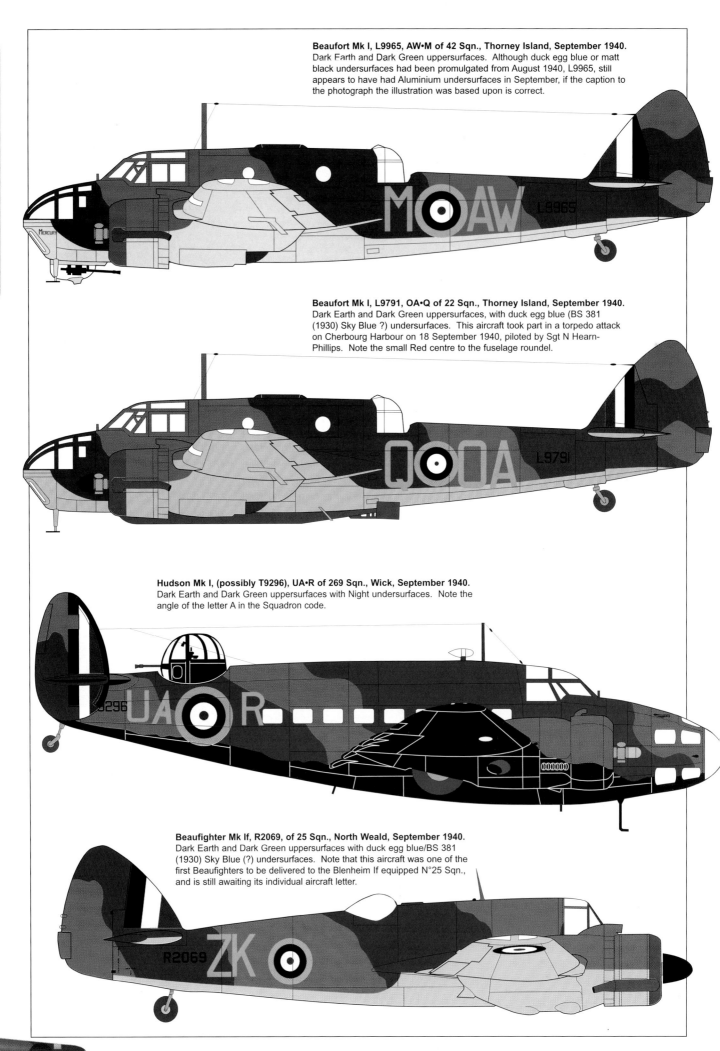

Beaufort Mk I, L9965, AW•M of 42 Sqn., Thorney Island, September 1940.
Dark Farth and Dark Green uppersurfaces. Although duck egg blue or matt black undersurfaces had been promulgated from August 1940, L9965, still appears to have had Aluminium undersurfaces in September, if the caption to the photograph the illustration was based upon is correct.

Beaufort Mk I, L9791, OA•Q of 22 Sqn., Thorney Island, September 1940.
Dark Earth and Dark Green uppersurfaces, with duck egg blue (BS 381 (1930) Sky Blue ?) undersurfaces. This aircraft took part in a torpedo attack on Cherbourg Harbour on 18 September 1940, piloted by Sgt N Hearn-Phillips. Note the small Red centre to the fuselage roundel.

Hudson Mk I, (possibly T9296), UA•R of 269 Sqn., Wick, September 1940.
Dark Earth and Dark Green uppersurfaces with Night undersurfaces. Note the angle of the letter A in the Squadron code.

Beaufighter Mk If, R2069, of 25 Sqn., North Weald, September 1940.
Dark Earth and Dark Green uppersurfaces with duck egg blue/BS 381 (1930) Sky Blue (?) undersurfaces. Note that this aircraft was one of the first Beaufighters to be delivered to the Blenheim If equipped N°25 Sqn., and is still awaiting its individual aircraft letter.

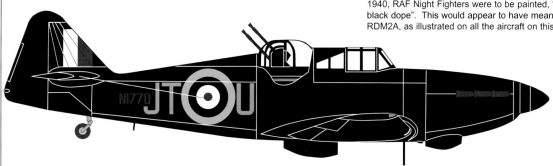

Defiant Mk I, N1770, JT•U of 256 Sqn., Catterick, winter 1940/41.
Following the decision at a meeting at the Air Ministry on 30 October 1940, RAF Night Fighters were to be painted, "special night flying black dope". This would appear to have meant Special Night RDM2A, as illustrated on all the aircraft on this page.

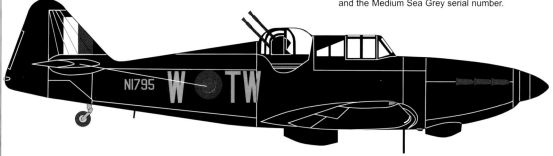

Defiant Mk I, N1795, TW•W of 141 Sqn., Gravesend, November 1940.
Special Night RDM2A overall. Note the toned-down fuselage roundel and the Medium Sea Grey serial number.

Beaufighter Mk If, R2059, A2 of the Fighter Interception Unit (FIU), Tangmere, September 1940.
Special Night RDM2A overall. Note the numeral 2 repeated on the engine cowling, and the large Red centre to the fuselage roundel.

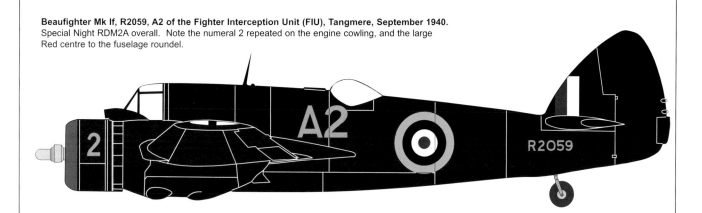

Beaufighter Mk If, R2101, NG•R of 604 (County of Middlesex) Sqn., Middle Wallop, winter 1940/41.
Special Night RDM2A overall. Note the large Medium Sea Grey code letters, and the numeral 3 on the engine cowling.

was originally designed to supersede.
There is no British Standard or Federal Standard match for this colour.

Sky

Introduced to the RAF as a whole from circa June 1940, it appears to have been the middle of September before its use as a camouflage colour on the undersurfaces of Day Fighters became widespread. Although it fell from use by the RAF post-war, its continuing use by Naval Aviation ensured that it was retained in the MoS colour range. Confusingly, the MoS range contains two versions of Sky, Aircraft Finish 9; and Aircraft Finish 9A. These colours are so similar as to be almost indistinguishable to the naked eye. It was Aircraft Finish 9A which was included in BS 381C in 1964 as No 210 Sky.
Colour matched by BS 381C No 210 Sky and FS 595B 34424

Aluminium

Until the introduction of Sky in 1940, this colour was often used on the undersurfaces of day flying aircraft in several roles.
There is no BS 381C match for this colour. Colour matched by FS 595B 17178

Identification Colours
Medium Sea Grey

The date of this colour's introduction remains unclear. Intended for use from about 1936, it would appear to have been in use by 1940. Medium Sea Grey was often referred to as Sea Grey Medium for much of its life, the change in terminology seems to have been made by the time AP 2656A was first issued in 1944. Medium Sea Grey was included in the post war MoS colour range as Aircraft Finish No 4. In 1964 Aircraft Finish No 4 Medium Sea Grey was one of the aircraft colours included in BS 381 as No 637.
Colour matched by BS 381C No 637 Medium Sea Grey. The closest FS 595 colour 36270

Red

This was the dull identification colour used in National markings from 1937 until the post-war roundel was introduced in 1947 when Bright Red replaced it. It then fell from use and was not included in the MoS colour range.
There is no match for this colour in BS 381C. The closest FS 595B colour is 30109

Bright Red

This was the pre-war bright red used in National markings. Supposedly superseded by Red from 1937, this colour continued to be used in National markings by some aircraft manufacturers such as Glosters until at least September 1940. Although apparently little used after 1940, this colour came back into use from 1947 onwards. As with Sky, the MoS colour range contained two versions of a bright red, both of which are simply named 'Red'; Aircraft Finish No 11, and Aircraft Finish No 11A. Like the two shades of Sky, it is almost impossible to see any difference between these two colours with the naked eye.

Neither one was ever incorporated into BS 381C apparently because both were almost identical to BS 381C 538 Post Office Red which has been in BS 381 since 1930. From 1966, AP 1086 Vocabulary of RAF Equipment, Section 33B, Aircraft Primers, Finishes, Paints and Associate Materials began to quote BS 381C colours for most of the top coat finish colours. This implies an apparent change in the nomenclature with the bright identification red which had previously been called 'Bright Red' now apparently being called Post Office Red 538. In more recent times the name of BS 381C 538 has been changed from 'Post Office Red' to 'Cherry'. The colour however, remains unaltered.
Colour matched by BS 381C No 538 Post Office Red/Cherry. The closest FS 595 colour is 11140

White

This was the traditional white identification colour used in National markings which was included in the MoS colour range as Aircraft Finish No 1A.. No white colour has ever been included in BS 381.
There is no BS 381C or FS 595 match for this colour.

Blue

This was the dull identification colour used in national markings from 1937 until the post-war roundel was introduced in 1947 when Bright Blue replaced it. It then fell from use and was not included in the MoS colour range.
There is no BS 381C match for this colour. The closest FS 595 colour is 35048.

Bright Blue

This was the pre-war bright blue used in the identification roundels. Supposedly superseded by Blue from 1937, this colour continued to be used in national markings by some aircraft manufacturers such as Glosters until at least September 1940. Although apparently little used after 1940, this colour came back into use from 1947 onwards. As with Sky and Bright Red, the MoS colour range contained two versions of a bright blue, both of which are simply named 'Blue'; Aircraft Finish No 12, and Aircraft Finish No 12A. Like the two shades of Sky and Bright Red, it is almost impossible to see any difference between these two colours with the naked eye. Neither one was ever incorporated into BS 381C. When AP 1086 began to quote BS 381C colours for most of the top coat finish colours in 1966, the bright identification blue which had previously been called 'Bright Blue' was now apparently being called Roundel Blue 110. This colour was added to the 1964 edition of BS 381C by Amendment No 1 dated 30 August 1966.
Colour matched by BS. 381C No 110 Roundel Blue. The closest FS 595 colour is 15056

'RAF pale blue'

Apparently the same pale blue as the RAF Ensign, this colour appears to have been used in small quantities in rank pennants. It does not appear to have a Standard, and no Stores Reference Number for it has yet

come to light. It would appear to be something like FS 595B 15450.

Yellow

Used in national markings from 1937 until 1947, this colour remained in use with the RAF post-war and was included in the MoS colour range as Aircraft Finish No 2. This colour appears to have a distinctly 'orange' cast to it which appears to have been lost from the later high gloss yellow MoS Aircraft Finish No 405 which appears to date from the mid-1950s. Neither Aircraft Finish No 2 nor Aircraft Finish No 405 were included in BS 381C. This might have been because by the time the MoS colours were included in BS 381C in 1964, Aircraft Finish No 405 had superseded Aircraft Finish No 2; and BS 381C No 356 Golden Yellow which had been in BS 381 since its first issue in 1930, might have been considered a close enough match to Aircraft Finish No 405 to make the latter colour's inclusion in BS 381C pointless.
There is no BS 381C match for this colour. The closest FS 595 colour is 33538.

Green

Whilst before the Second World War there was a standard issued by the Air Ministry for a colour called 'Identification Green', it seems to have fallen from use during the war. During 1940 it is likely that this colour was still available. Then it was probably something like BS 381C No 218 Grass Green, or FS 595B 14187.

A note on American aircraft paints

The subject of American colours applied to aircraft supplied to Britain would appear to be a subject in its own right on which little information appears to be available at the moment.

Aircraft ordered from the United States under Direct Purchase were painted in the United States before delivery, using paints which were required to be matched to the Air Ministry Standards. How closely these colours did match the British standards is not known, but it is currently assumed that those aircraft built to British orders up to and including 1940 were finished in colours which were specifically mixed to Air Ministry samples, and were presumably a very close match.

This situation might have begun to change as a result of the United States Government's decision to massively expand its own aircraft industry following Franklin D Roosevelt's call for the United States to "manufacture 50,000 aircraft per year" during the Presidential election campaign of 1940.

The shortages of materials that this produced across the American aircraft industry may have affected later deliveries, which might well have been finished in the closest colour available from stock, rather than using specially mixed and/or manufactured paints. For example, it is known that later in the war, the Bulletin 41 colour, Dark Olive Drab 41, replaced Dark Green on American aircraft supplied to Britain under Lend-Lease, and when initially applied, was a very near match.

Wellington Mk Ic, L7842, KX•T of 311 (Czecho-Slovak) Sqn., Honington, October 1940.
Dark Earth and Dark Green uppersurfaces with Special Night RDM2A undersurfaces and fuselage sides. Note how the White of the fuselage roundel has been painted over in Night.

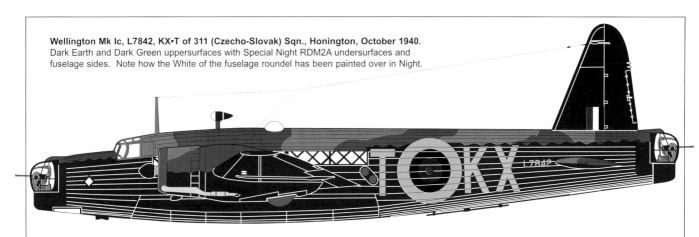

Hampden Mk I, P1228, ZN•L of 106 Sqn., Finningley, winter 1940/41.
Dark Earth and Dark Green uppersurfaces with Special Night RDM2A undersurfaces and fuselage sides. Note the toned-down fuselage roundel and fin stripes.

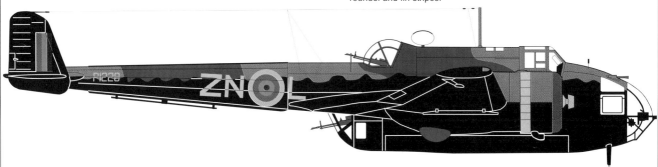

Defiant Mk I, N1572, KO•I of 2 Sqn., Clifton, September 1940.
Dark Earth and Dark Green uppersurfaces with duck egg green undersurfaces. This aircraft was undergoing trials to assess the type's suitability for Army Co operation work.

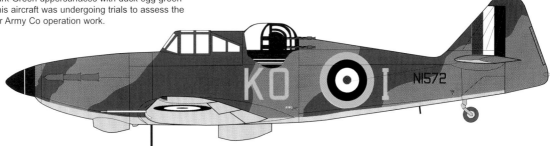

Lysander Mk II, P1674, HB•T of 239 Sqn., Hatfield, September 1940.
Dark Earth and Dark Green uppersurfaces with Sky undersurfaces. Note the large diameter fuselage roundel and the spacing of the code letters.

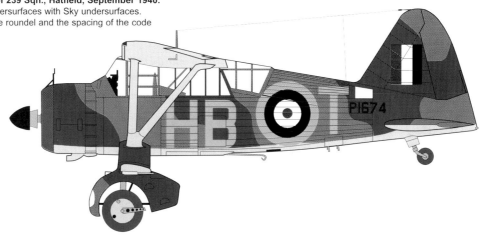

Dark Earth	Dark Green	Night / black	Sky	Duck Egg Green
Medium Sea Grey	Red	White	Blue	Yellow

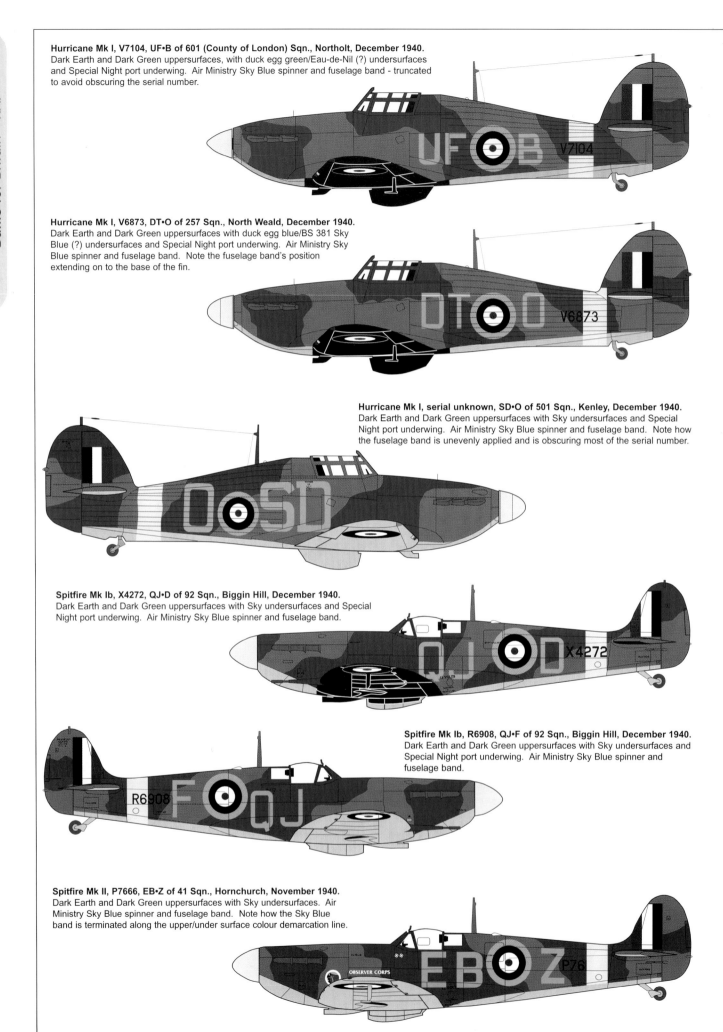

Hurricane Mk I, V7104, UF•B of 601 (County of London) Sqn., Northolt, December 1940.
Dark Earth and Dark Green uppersurfaces, with duck egg green/Eau-de-Nil (?) undersurfaces and Special Night port underwing. Air Ministry Sky Blue spinner and fuselage band - truncated to avoid obscuring the serial number.

Hurricane Mk I, V6873, DT•O of 257 Sqn., North Weald, December 1940.
Dark Earth and Dark Green uppersurfaces with duck egg blue/BS 381 Sky Blue (?) undersurfaces and Special Night port underwing. Air Ministry Sky Blue spinner and fuselage band. Note the fuselage band's position extending on to the base of the fin.

Hurricane Mk I, serial unknown, SD•O of 501 Sqn., Kenley, December 1940.
Dark Earth and Dark Green uppersurfaces with Sky undersurfaces and Special Night port underwing. Air Ministry Sky Blue spinner and fuselage band. Note how the fuselage band is unevenly applied and is obscuring most of the serial number.

Spitfire Mk Ib, X4272, QJ•D of 92 Sqn., Biggin Hill, December 1940.
Dark Earth and Dark Green uppersurfaces with Sky undersurfaces and Special Night port underwing. Air Ministry Sky Blue spinner and fuselage band.

Spitfire Mk Ib, R6908, QJ•F of 92 Sqn., Biggin Hill, December 1940.
Dark Earth and Dark Green uppersurfaces with Sky undersurfaces and Special Night port underwing. Air Ministry Sky Blue spinner and fuselage band.

Spitfire Mk II, P7666, EB•Z of 41 Sqn., Hornchurch, November 1940.
Dark Earth and Dark Green uppersurfaces with Sky undersurfaces. Air Ministry Sky Blue spinner and fuselage band. Note how the Sky Blue band is terminated along the upper/under surface colour demarcation line.

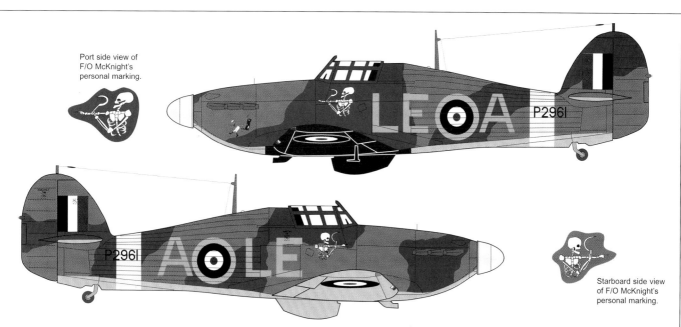

Port side view of
F/O McKnight's
personal marking.

Starboard side view
of F/O McKnight's
personal marking.

Hurricane Mk I, P2961, LE•A of 242 Sqn., Duxford, December 1940, flown by F/O W L 'Willie' McKnight.
Dark Earth and Dark Green uppersurfaces with duck egg green/Eau-de-Nil (?) undersurfaces and Special
Night port underwing. Air Ministry Sky Blue spinner and fuselage band.
Below, uppersurface camouflage pattern of P2961, to 'A Scheme'.

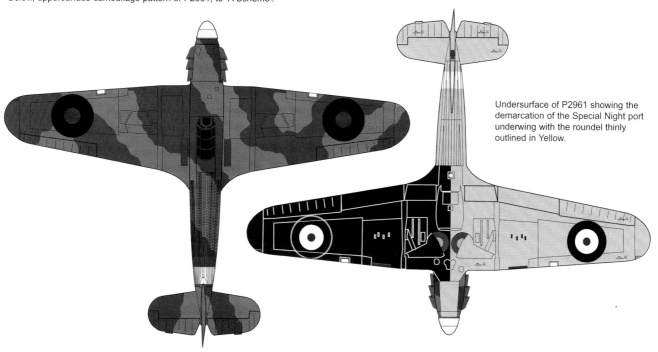

Undersurface of P2961 showing the
demarcation of the Special Night port
underwing with the roundel thinly
outlined in Yellow.

Variations in 18 inch wide tail band presentation

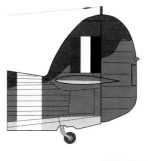
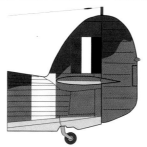

Dark Earth	Dark Green	Sky
Duck Egg Blue	Duck Egg Green	Sky Blue
Night / black	Medium Sea Grey	Red
White	Blue	Yellow

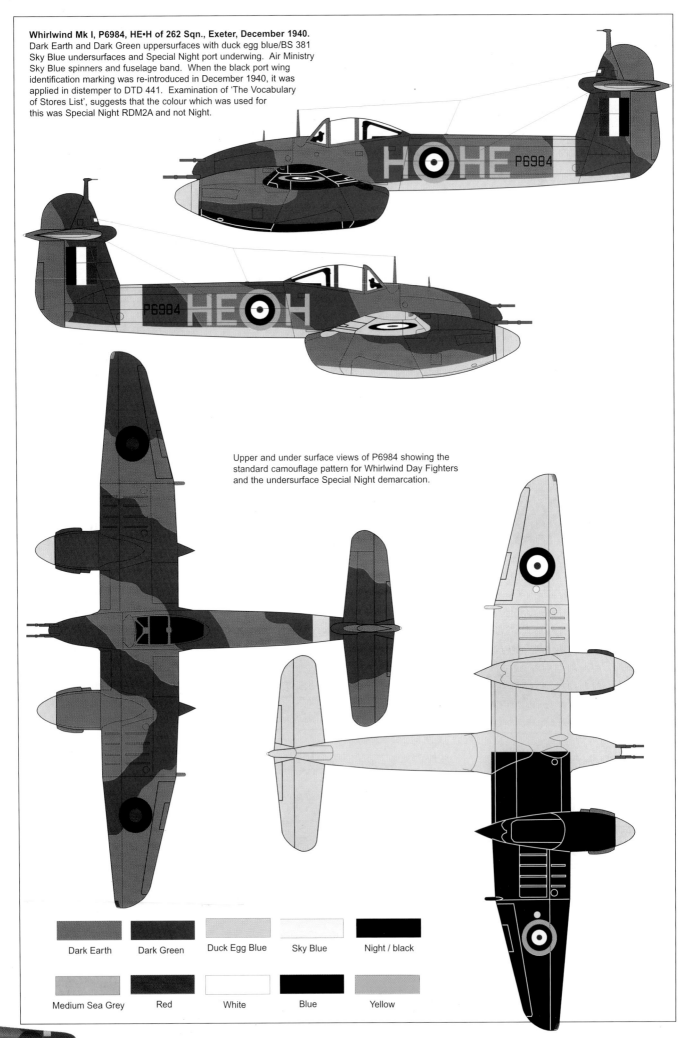

Whirlwind Mk I, P6984, HE•H of 262 Sqn., Exeter, December 1940.
Dark Earth and Dark Green uppersurfaces with duck egg blue/BS 381
Sky Blue undersurfaces and Special Night port underwing. Air Ministry
Sky Blue spinners and fuselage band. When the black port wing
identification marking was re-introduced in December 1940, it was
applied in distemper to DTD 441. Examination of 'The Vocabulary
of Stores List', suggests that the colour which was used for
this was Special Night RDM2A and not Night.

Upper and under surface views of P6984 showing the
standard camouflage pattern for Whirlwind Day Fighters
and the undersurface Special Night demarcation.

Dark Earth	Dark Green	Duck Egg Blue	Sky Blue	Night / black
Medium Sea Grey	Red	White	Blue	Yellow

9

10

11

12

13

14

15

16

9) Roundel from an unidentified Hurricane held at Shoreham Aircraft Museum in Kent. This unidentified Hurricane was lost whilst in the hands of 303 Sqn on 27 September 1940. Note that the yellow and white colours were marked first, and the red and blue applied over the top.

10) Close-up of the centre disc. The use of bright identification colours suggests that this was a Gloster-built machine. The Bright Blue was overpainted with Blue at some point. Close examination reveals a small hole in the centre of the roundel made by the compasses which were used to mark the roundel out.

11) Tailwheel and strut from Spitfire Mk I, X4325, held at Shoreham Aircraft Museum in Kent. This aircraft was delivered on 31 August 1940 and lost in the hands of 41 Sqn on 11 September. The colour of this artefact came as something of a surprise as it matched the colour Sky Grey.

12) Fabric covered elevator from an unidentified aircraft held at Brenzett Aeronautical Museum. This artefact was finished in Dark Earth and Dark Green on its uppersurfaces, and Sky Grey on its undersurfaces. Where the Sky Grey had flaked off, the original Aluminium finish was revealed.

13) Top of the rudder from an unidentified Spitfire held at Lashenden Air Warfare Museum. Colours present are Dark Earth and Dark Green camouflage, Night stencilling, red fabric tautening dope, and the manufacturer's plate.

14) Close-up of some of the stencilling which has been applied in Night. The letters are approximately one inch high, and three quarters of an inch in width. The letters 'CX' signify a proprietary Cellon doping treatment for fabric covered surfaces.

15) Close-up of the manufacturer's plate. This gives the date of this components completion as 15 March 1940, at Rochester in Kent.

16) The other side of the rudder revealed that after being doped with red primer, the whole surface was finished in Dark Earth before having the Dark Green applied over the top. Close examination shows the Dark Earth showing through where the Dark Green has been scratched off.

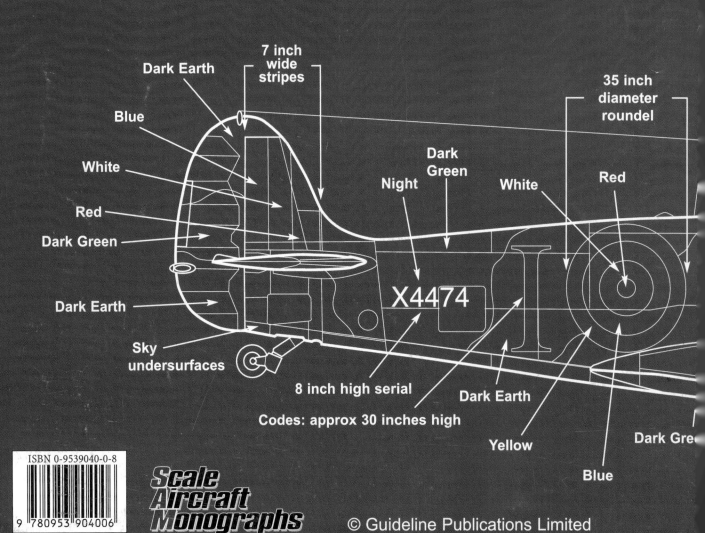

7 inch wide stripes

Dark Earth

Blue

White

Red

Dark Green

Dark Earth

Sky undersurfaces

35 inch diameter roundel

Night

Dark Green

White

Red

X4474

8 inch high serial

Codes: approx 30 inches high

Dark Earth

Yellow

Blue

Dark Gre

ISBN 0-9539040-0-8

9 780953 904006

Scale Aircraft Monographs

© Guideline Publications Limited